Needlework Nostalgia

Needlework Nostalgia

A COLLECTION OF AUTHENTIC
NEEDLEWORK DESIGNS FROM THE BUTTERICK ARCHIVES

Edited by Barbara Weiland

Butterick Publishing

Editor-in-Chief
Barbara Weiland

Research Consultant
Helen Cushman

Associate Editor
Evelyn Brannon

Technical Artist
Janet Lombardo

Copyright © 1975 by
BUTTERICK PUBLISHING
161 Sixth Avenue
New York, New York 10013

A Division of American Can

First Printing, April 1975
Second Printing, December 1975

Library of Congress Catalog Card Number 74-29072
International Standard Book Number 0-88421-021-9

ACKNOWLEDGEMENTS

Butterick Publishing wishes to thank the following individuals who generously donated their time to adapt, interpret, and execute the design samples which appear in color throughout *Needlework Nostalgia.*

Donna Ardito: Butterfly Jewel, **page 62.**

Pam Aulson: All Aboard, page 67.

Evelyn Brannon: Dinnertime and Feathered Friends, page 36; Oriental Medallion, page 11; Fancy Block Alphabet Evening Bag, page 6.

Mary Ann Drury: Balloons, page 62.

Carol Gull: Déco Rays, page 62; Rick Rack Napkin Rings, page 67.

Ann Hilburn: Morning Glories, page 6.

Janet Lombardo: Tango, page 6; Valentine Pincushion, page 67.

Bobbi Matela: Proud Parent, page 36; Peter Cottontail, Elephant Parade, Bird Talk, and A Squirrel's Christmas, page 67.

Marsha McCormick: Ebenezer Elephant, page 36.

Elaine Schmidt: Tulip Garden and Happy Heart, page 67; Cross-stitch Alphabet Quilt, page 46.

Harriet Sottile: Bartholomew Bunny, Floral Alphabet Napkin, and Christmas Bells Watchband, page 67; High Hatter (left) page 6; What's For Lunch, page 36.

Barbara Weiland: Sailing Ship, and Cheviots, page 36; Flower Patch Quilt, page 23; Cheviots, page 62; Chinese Patchwork, Centennial Patchwork, Mosaics, and Upsilon, page 11; High Hatter Pillow, page 6; Fruit and Flowers Watchband, page 67.

Alexandra Zois: Patriotic Eagle, cover design; High Hatter (right) page 6.

In addition we would like to thank the following companies for donating materials for some of the design samples.

Ameritex for the red/white and navy/white Malibu seersucker floral prints used in the Flower Patch Quilt pictured on page 23.

The Armo Company for Cut 'N Stuff used to fill all pillows.

The Pellon Corporation for the Polyester Fleece used to interline the Flower Patch Quilt pictured on page 23.

The Wm. E. Wright Company for the Needlepoint Watchbands which appear on page 67.

Color Photography by Laurence Cox

Book Design by Bob Antler

Preface

As Americans pause to take a long look back to their origins, it seems particularly appropriate to salute one aspect of that history which is, today receiving a great deal of attention. In this age of machines and mobility, a reverence for the artistry of old handcrafts, and in this case more specifically, of needlework in all its forms has spurred an unprecedented crafts revival. Needlepoint, patchwork, quilting, embroidery, and appliqué are once again the pastime of many Americans, men and women alike.

Needlework Nostalgia is an inspiring presentation of patterns for all of these art-needlework forms. The designs, which date from 1850 to 1930, were chosen from among thousands of possibilities in the cherished publications collected in the Butterick Archives. The patterns, sixty-five in all, range from patchwork designs of the 1800's to the bold geometrics of the Art Déco period. The backs of playing cards, a design for linoleum tile, 1920's fashion illustrations, reinterpretations of old Butterick needlework patterns, magazine cover designs, old monograms, and patterns first intended for crochet and cross-stitch—all have found their way to these pages for the fresh, contemporary interpretation of your needle. The final selection was difficult, to say the least, because there was so much from which to choose! Good design has a way of lasting forever and these are as timely today as they were when first conceived for their original purposes.

As you read the fascinating story of needlework in America and make your first design selection, remember that the full possibilities of any needlework design are seldom realized but all it takes is a little ingenuity and freedom from convention to adapt a pattern to almost any purpose. There is no limit to the use you can make of a design if you loosen the rein on your imagination. A patchwork pattern is not just a patchwork pattern nor is it limited to its original purpose as a quilt top. A needlepoint pillow or picture can just as easily evolve as can a patchwork pillow. And a beautiful floral embroidery design can be enlarged to become an appliqué or to be used as a quilting pattern. Cross-stitch, crochet, and knitting patterns which appear on a graph are easily translated in needlepoint, and monograms are no longer limited to napkins and scarves. An old alphabet originally intended for fancy beading is just as appropriate for cross-stitch in the squares of a checked gingham quilt.

Whatever you choose to do, the results can be truly distinctive and individual and heirlooms in their own right. Here, then, are the designs chosen for their timelessness and for their limitless suitability for a variety of needlework forms and interpretations. The whole sub-

*Needlework
Nostalgia*

ject of combining old designs and contemporary materials is a fascinating one and an inspiring exercise in creativity and self-expression. Several of the designs appear in graph form for needlepoint or cross-stitch and many more appear in a size suitable for tracing directly onto canvas or fabric. The history of each design is included for your enjoyment. And, you'll also find basic instructions for the needlework forms most appropriate for interpreting your design choice as well as suggestions and directions for finishing your nostalgic needlework with a high note of creative excitement.

A representative group of the designs were worked for your examination and appear in striking color photography. Color suggestions also appear on several of the individual design plates as well. Look for color ideas in everything you see—a bit of pretty silk ribbon from your scrap bag may be just the color inspiration you need.

As you scan these pages, I know you will find not one, but many designs that will appeal to your creative instincts and provide a pleasant occupation for whiling away the evening hours in front of a fire or for filling idle moments while the cookies bake or you wait for the dentist. The execution of these designs will provide you with pleasurable pursuits for years to come and the value of your finished work will far exceed that of any mass-produced item.

Barbara Weiland

Contents

1
Past Perspectives

The Romance of the Needle: A Brief History of Needlework in America

Perhaps you have one yourself—I have, a little brass bird that perches on the edge of my sewing-table and opens an obliging bill to hold my fancy work when I am embroidering. My grandmother used it when she worked on her samplers or hemstitched endless neck-cloths for her father. We have some of her handiwork still and the small painstaking stitches are at once my envy and despair. There is something so calm, so leisurely, so unhurried about them that I frequently experience a slight feeling of regret when I look from them to my own sewing done at odd minutes between a dozen pressing engagements, sometimes by my own fireside, sometimes under the electric light of a Pullman compartment on a hasty trip across country to a horse show or an aviation meet. But it is a feeling that soon passes, for imperfect as my own work is beside the fine, close-set stitches of a half century ago, it has its own beauty and charm with its gay colors and its bold, flaunting outlines . . . . It really gives a very definite purpose to the prettiest and pleasantest of

pastimes when you know that your fancy work is going toward the beautifying of your home or the curtailing of expense in regard to your own and your children's wardrobes. It more than justifies all the lazy, restful hours you spend on your own veranda or before your fire at work on nothing more exacting than a bit of lace or embroidery.

Helen Berkeley-Loyd
"Butterick Designs," 1911.

Although Ms. Berkeley-Loyd penned these words in the early part of the twentieth century, they are the sentiments echoed across centuries by needlewomen who recognized the timeliness and intrinsic value of needlework, so aptly named "fancy work" by our great grandmothers.

Specifically, needlework is embroidery, but today, in its broadest sense, it has come to include other forms of needlework, some of which have existed since human beings first experienced the desire to embellish themselves and their surroundings for purely decorative reasons. Embroidery, quilting, appliqué, patchwork, and needlepoint all have their roots in the development of the textile industry by ancient civilizations along the

1

banks of the Ganges, Euphrates, and Nile. The ornamentation of woven fabrics probably experienced rudimentary development in ancient Egypt and was later perfected in Asia Minor before it reached European civilization through the ancient cultures of Greece and Rome.

All forms of needlework flourished in Europe during the Middle Ages. Embroidery, for instance, reached such a state of perfection that guilds of "embroiderers" were established to insure the high quality of this fine needlework. The art of needlework was encouraged, prized, and well paid for in England and abroad. Records show that the English monarchs commissioned various works of embroidery for state gifts or for their personal use. In 1480, Martin Jumbard, embroiderer, was paid fourpence for embroidering eight large roses, and one penny each for forty-eight small roses, the value of a penny in those days being comparable to the British pound of today with allowances made for differences in the standards of living.

By the seventeenth century, the most common forms of needlework practiced today had reached their peak and the skills inherent to each were carried to America by colonists eager to build new lives in their "promised land." The hardships experienced during their first years are witnessed·in the adaptation of these prized needlework skills to necessity. The early settlers, expecting to find the warm weather of Virginia throughout the area along the mid-Atlantic seaboard where they made their homes were ill-prepared to survive the harsh weather and privations of the first years in their new surroundings. Clothing and quilts, painstakingly prepared before the voyage to the New World, were worn to near shreds and since a colonial textile industry was not yet established, fabrics were scarce and, when available, quite expensive. Necessity was truly the "mother of invention," and the purely American craft, the patchwork quilt, evolved from the need to keep warm, even when fabrics were not available for new clothing and bedding.

The Patchwork Quilt

As romantic as Colonial American history may seem as we look back on it, life in the colonies was a challenge to the bravery and the ingenuity of the colonial housewife whose main concern was the welfare and survival of her family. Provisions for warmth were of utmost concern during the cold New England winters and when the clothing and quilts brought from Europe began to show signs of wear, she began to patch them together with scraps of fabric and the remains of clothing, until new ones could be made from fabrics brought from England. When even these haphazardly patched-together· quilts were too worn to keep anyone warm, they were used for the inner layers of new quilts, pieced

together by Puritan women from the scraps left on the tables and floor after garments were cut from precious new cloth. The first new quilts made in America were most likely filled with grasses and corn husks and the layers held together with twine pulled through and tied in knots.

Unwittingly, the colonial housewife had initiated a new art form, the American patchwork quilt, inherent to American ingenuity, efficiency, economy, and practicality. Yes, these women had learned the art of quilting in Europe, but the heritage of European quilting was in appliquéd quilts. These were constructed by cutting design shapes from fabrics (typically, Indian chintzes) and then applying them to a solid white quilt top before securing the layers with tiny, painstaking quilting stitches. When fabrics became more widely available in the late eighteenth and nineteenth centuries, American appliquéd quilts, closely akin to the European quilt, were again in vogue. But in the meantime, old became new as tiny pieces of dressmaking scraps and the breeches too worn in the seat for repair made their way into the intricate patterns of American colonial patchwork which evolved, in time, from haphazard patching to carefully planned works of art accomplished by "piecing" together small pieces of fabric to form repeated, overall geometric patterns.

With the development of this American homecraft came a new social convention, the quilting bee. Confined by inclement weather and muddy roads during the winter months, the American woman spent her free minutes by the fireside making patchwork quilt tops and eagerly awaiting the spring thaw which would inevitably bring wagonloads of neighbors for the first social activity of the season. In addition to the utilitarian pupose of the quilting bee (the actual work of quilting) it was a time for a little frivolity—for dressing up a bit, for gossiping, and for romancing. Men, women, and children alike came from miles around, the men to "raise" a new barn or to hold a husking bee, the women to talk while their fingers flew, exchanging new recipes and new designs for patchwork, the children to play beneath the quilting frames and catch bits of the latest grown-up gossip. The day was concluded with a hearty evening meal, games, and a little dancing before the journey home.

Tradition, symbolism, and superstition were woven into the very fabric of old quilts. The Pennsylvania Dutch, who were (and still are) considered the most accomplished and original quiltmakers, believed that a perfectly made quilt displeased and insulted God. For this reason, their quilts are characterized by a "mistake" made on purpose. Quilts were ever-present in the thoughts of young girls. The traditions and superstitions surrounding the "bridal quilt" were carried from Europe to the colonies. An American girl, taught to sew at a very early age, was expected to complete at least a dozen quilts by the time she was wed. At a quilting bee where her engagement was announced, the bridal quilt top was made and appliquéd with hearts and lovers' knots, motifs reserved exclusively for this quilt (it was bad luck to use these symbols until the engagement was official). Quilts were of such importance that they were often included in wills and in marriage inventories.

After the War for Independence, the traditions of quilting were carried to new lands as Americans began the westward expansion that added new territories and eventually new states to the fledgling nation. Old quilting patterns were carried with them and new ones developed and were named for the people, places, and events that colored their long journey. During all this time the appliquéd quilt was called the "good quilt" and was reserved for company or for the bridal chest. Appliqué, with its roots in the European Middle Ages, is considered a variety of patchwork although it really preceded the development of American patchwork.

With freedom from English iron-rule, the American textile industry had a chance to develop and flourish. With the wider availability of fabric, the necessity for piecing and patching quilts together diminished and in the nineteenth century quilting, patchwork, and appliqué, so closely intertwined, became leisure-time activities rather than completely necessary work. Appliquéd quilts were more abundant and in some quilts attention was focused more on the intricacy and number of stitches than on piecing colored scraps together. The all-white quilt with a pattern of thousands of tiny stitches holding the layers together evolved at this time. Trapunto or Italian quilting was also popular. This type of quilting consisted of two or more layers of fabric with a pattern worked in tiny running stitches which was stuffed through a slit made in the back layer to produce a high relief design on the surface.

Embroidery and Needlepoint

Patchwork, appliqué, and quilting, while perhaps the most utilitarian of needlework forms in their ultimate product, were not the only practiced needle arts in America. The development of American embroidery closely parallels that of the patchwork quilt for it was influenced by the same hardships and privations as well as the same background. The colonists reached America with a rich heritage of needlework. Needle art forms had reached their height of perfection in Europe during the Middle Ages. The skills were known to most American settlers but the scarcity of yarns and materials and the lack of time created the very essence of American embroidery which was one of the chief means for enlivening and brightening a home in the colonies since print fabrics were not easily come by. It was done in stolen moments before the fire at night when the family was in bed because the essential spinning, dyeing,

weaving, and sewing took most of the housewife's time during the day. Scarcity of yarns played a major role in the development of American embroidery designs. Only the most economical stitches (those that took the least amount of yarn) were used and the embroidery was characterized by fresh, happy motifs—the sheep in the fields and the chickens at the back door—motifs that captured the things closest to home and the pastoral nature of life.

Some of the most treasured examples of early embroidery are the samplers worked by young girls. A sampler was one of the most important pieces of needlework a young girl executed. Once completed, it served as a pattern book of the most useful embroidery stitches. They were usually worked on a length of linen fabric and included such things as the alphabet and numbers, a short original poem, or a motto designed to instill a particular virtue in the worker. These early samplers are of increasing value today and are often found in museum collections of early American needlework artifacts.

A great deal of early American embroidery took the form of crewel-work, embroidery worked with a fine two-ply wool yarn. Crewel-work dates as far back as the 5th Century A.D. in the Orient. It was used extensively in Europe to depict scenes of historical and social significance as well as for the embellishment of religious vestments. But in America, crewel-work was characterized by a simple, homespun look rather than one of historical, religious, or social significance. Bedspreads and bed hangings, wing chairs, fine furniture, linens, and even petticoats were objects for "needle painting" with embroidery. Its true merit was that it was a relatively quick way to enhance an article with color and design since the plain background fabric was complete in itself.

Needlepoint was a form of needlework that experienced slow development in the New World. Needlepoint is embroidery worked with a needle and yarn over the counted threads of fabric. It was known in Europe and was often done to imitate the beautiful woven tapestries of the Middle Ages. As with all other needlecrafts, materials for needlepoint were scarce, and since steel tapestry needles were quite expensive and needlepoint required even more yarn than did crewel embroidery, it was not often practiced in the early days. It was considered frivolous and time-consuming in comparison to the other more necessary needle arts. A patchwork quilt kept one warm and could be completed in a few days, especially with the help of a quilting bee, but needlepoint was the fancy work of "ladies" who had little else to do with their time.

The Advent of the Machine Age

During the first seventy-five years of the nineteenth century, American needlework continued to flourish and became more and more extravagant as newer and better fabrics and yarns were increasingly available. A quilt of "white and rose colored satin" was displayed in 1876 at the United States Centennial Exhibition. On its white ground were embroidered 1500 roses and rosebuds and in each of these there were from 500 to 900 stitches. Seven thousand skeins of silk were used in the work and the lady who made it spent eighteen months at work on it.

This century was also marked by the advent of the Machine Age which is said by many to have dealt a cruel death blow to American creativity in needlework. Needlepoint was probably the first form to fall prey to the machine. In the latter part of the eighteenth century, stiff machine-made needlepoint canvas as we know it today was introduced. Then in 1803 a Berlin print seller had the idea to create printed needlepoint designs on paper. The designs were etched on copper plates in a grid pattern, printed, and painstakingly hand-colored. By 1820 these patterns were readily available to the masses. The designs were characterized by stereotyped florals worked in garish, bright colors with black the most popular color for the background. Needlepoint became known as "Berlin Work" and continued as such for over fifty years. Yarns colored with aniline dyes became available at about the same time as Berlin patterns and were used to execute the patterns on canvas. The Berlin patterns made needlepoint available and appealing to a mass market just as machinery would make other forms of needlework available to a mass market.

Many historians are quick to criticize the needlewomen of the centennial period for their infatuation with machine-made products and their monotonous copying of mass-produced designs with little evidence of true creativity. But can one really blame their enthusiasm when one considers that up until mechanization everything was done by hand? Machine-made goods replaced those which demanded hours of painstaking handwork. The one creative product that emerged from the Victorian era was the "crazy quilt." Often called a slumber robe or couch throw, this quilt was pieced together with odd scraps of velvet, silks, and other fancy fabrics, then elaborately embroidered and often hand-painted. Although these quilts appear to be haphazard arrangements of scraps, close examination indicates that this arrangement was probably carefully planned. Crazy quilts, considered collectors items today, were so delicate and fragile that they were rarely used. The evolution of American quiltmaking had come to a halt. Early quilts, although not at all decorative, were useful for keeping warm. Then evolved the patchwork quilt, a work of art in addition to a functional bed covering. And finally the crazy quilt, beautiful to behold with little, if any, utilitarian purpose.

The Emerging Revival

The Industrial Revolution placed American handicrafts in a secondary position. For example, knowing how to quilt became a sign of poverty. Quilting did experience a short-lived revival during the Depression but it was not until just recently, that the true value of needlework in all its forms was again recognized. Today, infatuation with mass-produced items has been replaced with a reverence for creative self-expression as witnessed in the current unprecedented revival of all forms of needlework. The contemporary emphasis is on good workmanship and the creative and innovative use of color and materials. Old designs in a contemporary translation combine to fulfill two current needs, identity with the past through the execution and updating of basic needlework forms and the desire to use one's hands to create something of lasting personal value.

With materials and instruction readily available, learning any or all of the needle crafts discussed here is feasible and accessible to almost anyone. Needlework provides a relaxing and productive activity which appeals to all ages and to men and women alike. It requires only a bit of patience and some esthetic sense. In our hurry-up-and-wait world, needlework projects can grow under your hands in no time at all while you wait in the dentist's office, ride on a bus or in a car, visit with neighbors, or watch television in the waning evening hours.

The evolution of needlework in the twentieth century is marked by the unrestricted use of each needlework form resulting in new end products. Quilting, patchwork, and appliqué are no longer confined to the production of quilts. Instead they are used separately or in combination to produce appliquéd shirts and pillows, elaborate quilted wall hangings, and patchwork bags, hats, even slipcovers. Needlepoint is no longer restricted to the floral footstools of the Victorian era. Stuffed needlepoint toys, Christmas tree ornaments, and tennis racquet covers are subjects for needlepoint. Even a needlepoint backgammon board is not unheard of. Belts, watchbands and entire garments cannot escape the creative whims of the needleworker. Almost any design can be interpreted in more than one needlework form depending on the skills and needs of the maker.

As in the past, contemporary needlework continues to provide a creative outlet which reflects the taste, manners, and customs of the changing American scene. It is one way in which the thoughts, philosophies, ideas, and knowledge of this generation can be preserved to make a lasting statement for future generations about the times in which we live.

The Design Sources

The collection of authentic designs between these covers represents only a small sampling of designs from an unending source of inspiration in the Butterick Archives. The designs in the collection cover the period from 1855 to 1930, a seventy-five year span that saw many changes in artistic style. They were selected from among thousands that appeared in such magazines as *Godey's Lady's Book, Peterson's,* and *The Delineator* and from *Butterick Designs*, Butterick's *Needle-Art*, and two rare, early needlework books, *Needle and Brush*, and *Artistic Alphabets* published by Butterick in the late 1880's.

Godey's is perhaps the best known of the women's magazines published in the nineteenth century. It was the first of its kind in the United States and provided American women with a glimpse of Paris in colored fashion plates which appeared in the front of each issue. (Women were paid a penny a sheet to watercolor these pages by hand.) Sarah Josepha Hale (1788-1879) wrote and edited much of the magazine over a fifty year period, aiding with distinction, the cause of women's rights.

Like *Godey's, Peterson's Magazine* brought French fashions to its audience from 1842 until it ceased publication (as did *Godey's*) in 1898, the same year that the Spanish American War broke out. *Peterson's* fashion plates entitled "Les Modes Parisiennnes" appeared as hand-colored, steel engravings accompanied by intricate fashion information. (It must be remembered that until the invention of the tissue paper pattern by Ebenezer Butterick in 1863, clothing was sewn from the pictures and descriptions in these and other magazines and from costumed dolls that originated in France in the seventeenth century.)

Peterson's and *Godey's* provided interesting reading for the day and had a little of everything: music, humorous sketches, romantic love stories, cultural features, recipes, household hints and projects for "the work basket." In 1876, if you subscribed to *Peterson's Magazine,* you could keep up with a "goose-pimply" historical novel called *The Days of Seventy-Six.*

> ... the military officer ... carried Rhoda Clyde ... and mounted the stairs swiftly, as if the girl were but a child in his arms. The flash of his epaulets, and the ring of his gilt spurs on the stairs, checked the crowd ... A scarcely perceptible quiver of the white eyelids, that swept the whiter cheeks with their lashes, and a faint stir of breath, perhaps between the painted lips, had brought swift enlightenment to his evil heart, and kindled it with audacity. Clasping his arms more tightly, he bent forward, and kissed those lips once and again ....

Pretty racy for straight-laced Victorian parlors!

Another issue gives us a glimpse of Victorian music. A bit of nostalgia called "Pull Down the Blind" is a ditty about a young lady whose first words when her boyfriend came to the house were,

> Pull down the blind,
> Pull down the blind;
> Pull down the blind, love
> come don't be unkind.
> Though we're alone, bear this in mind
> Somebody's looking, love,
> Pull down the blind.

In 1875, Butterick began to publish its answer to *Godey's* and *Peterson's. The Delineator* (named for a tailor's expansible pattern for cutting garments of various sizes) contained sketches of Butterick patterns in the latest styles. In the late 1800's *The Delineator* was primarily a fashion magazine with occasional sections devoted to needlework projects. An especially beautiful quilt design included here came from the pages of an 1881 issue of this magazine. *The Delineator* was characterized by elegant woodcuts and rare color prints with a minimum of advertising. From 1907 to 1910 with Theodore Dreiser as its editor, the magazine was used as a medium for articles on social reform, woman's suffrage, children's welfare, divorce, and the high cost of living as well as the latest information on fashion. As the years passed, *The Delineator* took on the characteristics of current ladies' magazines and included works of good fiction by such writers as John Galsworthy, Kathleen Norris, and Edgar Wallace. Several Art Déco designs in this book were chosen from the story and feature illustrations in the 1920 to 1930 issues of *The Delineator.*

Magazines about needlework flourished during the early twentieth century. In 1910, the editor of one of Butterick's early needlework magazines had this to say about the importance of needlework.

> Every woman who wants to be well-dressed ought always to keep a bit of embroidery or lace work in her sewing bag that she can pick up at odd moments and drop for days at a time if need be. You will find that it will grow under your hands without any effort whatsoever on your part.

Most of the designs in this book which date from 1900 to 1930 are brought to you here from the pages of Butterick's *Needle-Art, Butterick Designs,* and *Butterick Transfers,* magazines that illustrated Butterick's available needlework patterns and also contained designs and complete instructions for every imaginable type of needlework from embroidery to knitting to fabric stencilling.

The publications from which our designs were carefully selected are all collectors' items today. The legacy of their designs is yours for contemporary interpretation in *Needlework Nostalgia.*

A Word About Art Déco

Throughout this collection of designs for needlework are scattered a number of patterns that recall the forms, shapes, and motifs of Art Déco, an art style that reached its peak sometime between 1920 and 1930. This art style has been described as "chic," "streamlined," "fantastic," "eclectic," "flashy," and even "bizarre" depending on the eye of the beholder. Today, in the mid-1970's, objects rendered in this style have become true "collectibles" akin to real antiques (objects at least one hundred years of age).

In its various manifestations, Art Déco reflected influences from Cubism, the Russian Ballet, the pre-Columbian art of the Ancient Aztec, and the culture of ancient Egypt. Our design for *Shadow Cat* on page 44 is an excellent example of Egyptian influence in this art style. In its late stages, Art Déco expressed the era of the machine. In its own time it was known as the "modernist" or "modernistic" style, a term that was used as early as 1918 in Butterick fashion magazines. "Art moderne," "constructivist machine style," and "zig-zag moderne" were other descriptions commonly used.

The arrival of Art Déco is generally considered to have occured in 1925 when many examples were exhibited at the Exposition Internationale des Arts Décoratifs Industriels Modernes in Paris. Its shock effect was often greeted with a shudder, especially by those who still yearned for the romantic tendrils of Art Nouveau (*Morning Glories* on page 29 is an excellent example of this romantic art style). The sunburst was typically Art Déco, a motif said to have reflected the cult of sunbathing that arrived in the 1920's and recalled the sun-worship of Ancient Peru and Ancient Egypt.

Zig-zag designs from the art of pre-Columbian cultures were also characteristic. Ziggurats were everywhere—in the skylines of skyscrapers, in the lines of furniture. They were used as decoration on almost anything. (A ziggurat was a terraced temple tower, pyramidical in form. Ziggurats in Art Déco designs appeared as one side of one of these pyramids.) In industrial design, Art Déco can be characterized as the period of streamlining. Streamlined design was applied to objects never intended for speed: stoves, refrigerators, toasters, even linoleum designs. Surviving architectural examples of the Art Déco style include Radio City Music Hall, the Chrysler Building and the Chanin Building, all in New York City, and the Richfield Building in Los Angeles.

Art Déco was jazzy. It was Borzoi dogs, Ruhlmann furniture, the Chrysler Airflow, fashions with dropped waistlines and jagged hemlines, magazine covers by Erté, and a chaise lounge covered with imitation zebra skin. As for color schemes, Art Déco was a black-enamelled and chrome era. Aggressive, clashing colors like chartreuse, electric blue, hot pink, and blazing orange were characteristic.

The examples of Art Déco design included here come from the world of advertising, fashion, and magazine illustration. They did not originate as needlework patterns and are included for your interpretation in contemporary or Art Déco color schemes. They represent Art Déco in several of its phases, from the elegant, feminine version of its early beginnings to its stark geometric forms of the 1930's.

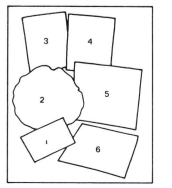

2 The Nostalgic Designs and Their Origins

AMERICANA

PATRIOTIC EAGLE, *design plate, page 12; cover design.*

America's Centennial year was one of celebration commemorating the 100th Anniversary of the signing of the Declaration of Independence. A number of beautiful pieces of needlework remain from that festive year; all are collectors'. items today. This design for a "Centennial Tidy in Crochet" appeared in the July, 1876 issue of *Peterson's Magazine.* (A "tidy" was a light, detachable covering used to protect the back or arm of a sofa from dirt and wear.)

The "Patriotic Eagle," interpreted for our cover in needlepoint on #10 canvas for Bicentennial needlework days, appeared on a Massachusetts penny in 1776, and in 1867 was adopted as the emblem of the United States. The design includes a shield and two flags representing the thirteen stars and stripes of the original colonies. The leaves are stylized renditions. Typically they would have been elm, beech, chestnut, or horse chestnut, though they could also be the laurel, sacred to the ancient Greeks and symbol of victory. If you interpret these as laurel leaves, you might like to include a few red berries among the green.

VALENTINE, *design plate, page 13; photo, page 67.*

Roses were among the most popular designs for the new craze of Berlin work that caught on in America in the 1800's. Berlin work was the faddish name for what is needlepoint today. In 1859, *Peterson's Magazine* printed this pattern for a lady's slipper (the heart shape was the toe, the bands the side of the slipper). Work it today in petit point (20 mesh/inch) with embroidery floss for a delicate pincushion like ours. Back it with felt or a scrap of velveteen and stuff tightly with fiberfill— or—use dried rose petals for a pretty sachet. Worked on #10 canvas as shown on the design plate it's the perfect size for a Valentine to send to someone special. Or try cross-stitch on gingham checks. The band of roses would make an especially nice bookmark or the border on a picture frame.

ALL ABOARD, *design plate, page 14; photo, page 67.*

Travelling days began in earnest for Americans when the steam engine effectively replaced the stagecoach. Today's handbag was yesterday's "railway bag" in which to carry on the trip one's needlework, scent bottle, and personal necessities. In a rare little needlepoint design from *Peterson's Magazine* of 1867 then, as now, we remember the shriek of the whistle, the chug of steam, as the conductor calls "All aboard."

To make a travelling bag like ours, you will need 1/2 yard of #10 needlepoint canvas, Persian yarn in seven colors, 1/2 yard velveteen, 1/2 yard lining fabric, and 54″ of decorative drapery cord. Make one complete tracing of the pattern on the design plate on tracing paper. Mark dotted lines and label as shown on design plate. Flip paper and transfer tracing to reverse side of paper. Position dotted line A on tracing over dotted line A on design plate and trace remainder of pattern. Position needlepoint canvas over tracing and transfer to canvas. Locate center of design and work train car from graph. Complete design areas working background last. Block finished needlepoint (page 83), trim margins to 1″, then construct bag. Cut backing of velveteen using original pattern plus 1″ seam allowances all around. With right sides together, stitch backing to needlepoint (1″ seam allowances) leaving the opening extension unstitched. Stitch again just inside the first row of stitching. If desired, insert matching cording (see page 95) in this seam before stitching. Trim seams to 3/8″ and clip curves carefully. Turn right side out and turn in opening extensions and tack in place. Securely tack two pieces of drapery cord (each 27″ long) inside bag at each end of opening. Cut two lining pieces and construct in same manner as bag. Turn inside out, insert in bag and slip stitch in place being sure to cover drapery cord ends.

FLOWER PATCH QUILT, *design plate, pages 15, 26, 27, 30, and 31; photo, page 23.*

This beautiful quilt pattern first appeared in *The Delineator* for April, 1881. In the original quilt, floral satin ribbons and silk embroidery surrounded the strong geometric center of silk triangles. Our translation is truly Americana in red, white, and blue prints and solids with crewel embroidery in each corner.

To make this quilt you will need:

2-1/2 yards 45″ white cotton broadcloth; cut four 13″ squares and 108 triangles using template on design plate.

2 yards 45″ red cotton broadcloth; cut 108 triangles.

2-1/4 yards 45″ red floral print and 2-1/2 yards 45″ blue floral print; from each print, cut two strips 7″ x 55″ and two strips 7″ x 73″.

5 yards 45″ blue and white polka dot cotton; divide yardage in half and seam together lengthwise. Cut down to 79″ x 97″.

1 yard 45″ blue and white polka dot cotton; cut into strips 3″ wide for binding.

Quilt batting and blue yarn for tying.

Embroider floral design(s) on each of the four 13″ squares.

Piece triangles together with 18 triangles (9 red and 9 white) across and 24 triangles down (12 red and 12 white).

Piece floral strips together as shown in photograph (page 23).

Then stitch strips, squares, and patchwork together using 1/2″ seam allowances. Layer and baste quilt top, batting, and backing together, then tie quilt with yarn at the corners of each square. (See pages 88 and 89.) Bind outer edges with strips of polka dot cotton.

UPSILON, *design plate, page 16; photo, page 11.*

"Upsilon" . . . the Greek symbol for our letter Y was known as early as 3000 B.C. in ancient Egypt. In 1889, a Victorian lady used the ancient symbol to beautify her home working it in velvet appliqué on a satin sofa pillow. One version showed it heavily embellished with silk embroidery in the fashion of the popular "Crazy Quilt" of the period. Our contemporary interpretation in an appliquéd pillow (18″ x 18″) requires 2/3 yard corduroy for the pillow background and backing, 2-1/2 yards cording, and a few scraps of coordinated printed fabric. It would be beautiful as a full-size quilt, too. See "Needlework Materials and Techniques" for appliqué instructions.

SUNBURST, *design plate, page 17.*

In 1888, *The Delineator* featured a design that was forty years ahead of its time yet as traditional as ancient Egypt. Distinctly Art Déco in feeling it might as easily have come from F. Scott Fitzgerald's *Great Gatsby* era as from the "Elegant Eighties." Yet the sun as a theme for artistic interpretation is as old as man. It originally appeared as a half sunburst in each square of a quilt; suggested colors were black velvet for the background and shades of orange for the sun. Try it as originally intended in the squares of a quilt or complete the circle and make a square pillow using either patchwork or appliqué techniques. Add the central rays with an embroidery stitch. The design template shows one corner (1/4) of a 12″ square.

CHINESE PATCHWORK, *design plate, page 19; photo, page 11.*

The star motif is a recurring one in traditional American patchwork patterns. In this bold design printed in 1859, the star appears again as a "pattern lately brought out in London which is called the Chinese Pattern."

Peterson's recommended it as a "striking design for a table cover or counterpane." Imagine it today as the central design on a circular tablecloth with matching chair cushions. To imitate the original pattern which called for a great proportion of black, we chose a colorful print on a black ground and coordinated it with gingham and plain colors. Once pieced together in true patchwork fashion, the "star" was machine-appliquéd to a 30" square of black hopsacking trimmed with a coordinating 2" band, then made into a pillow. (See directions for pillows on page 91.)

MOSAICS, *design plate, page 18; photo, page 11.*

In 1871, ten years before either Braque or Picasso was born, *Peterson's* published this cubistic design for patchwork to be done in velvets and satins with the small squares embroidered after the piecing was completed. Another design for patchwork shown in a later issue combined the same elements in a slightly different arrangement also given on the design plate. Experiment with these two shapes (triangles and squares) to develop a new mosaic, or interpret the original design in patchwork with appliquéd squares as a pillow, an entire quilt, or as placemats.

CENTENNIAL PATCHWORK, *design plate, page 20; photo, page 11.*

Gingham, dotted Swiss, and a floral print combine in a patriotic patchwork design that appeared in *Peterson's Magazine* in 1876, and was originally intended for interpretation in silks and velvets.

To duplicate it, use the templates on the design plate to cut six large squares and twenty-four small squares. Appliqué to a rectangle of background fabric (13-1/2" x 19"). Prepare a ruffle (2-1/2" finished width) following instructions on page 95, then assemble pillow top with ruffle and pillow backing using 1/2" seam allowances. (See page 91 for pillow instructions.)

OPTICAL BLOCKS, *design plate, page 21.*

This important and traditional patchwork design appeared in *Godey's Lady's Book* in 1858. Its optical effect is dramatic and modern to late twentieth century eyes. It is closely related to another very popular patchwork design known as "Baby's Blocks." For a striking effect, translate it in three intensities or values of a single color or try it in calico and ginghams.

"Optical Blocks" is a strong geometric design just as easily translated in needlepoint as in patchwork. In fact, this same design appeared in 1872 as a needlepoint slipper pattern for "the little folk [who] often want to do something for papa, in the way of a Christmas or New Year's gift."

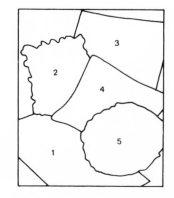

All designs which appear on graphs were done in the scale of 10 stitches per inch. Designs may be worked on any size canvas but size of completed work will change accordingly.

For graph color key, see page 82.

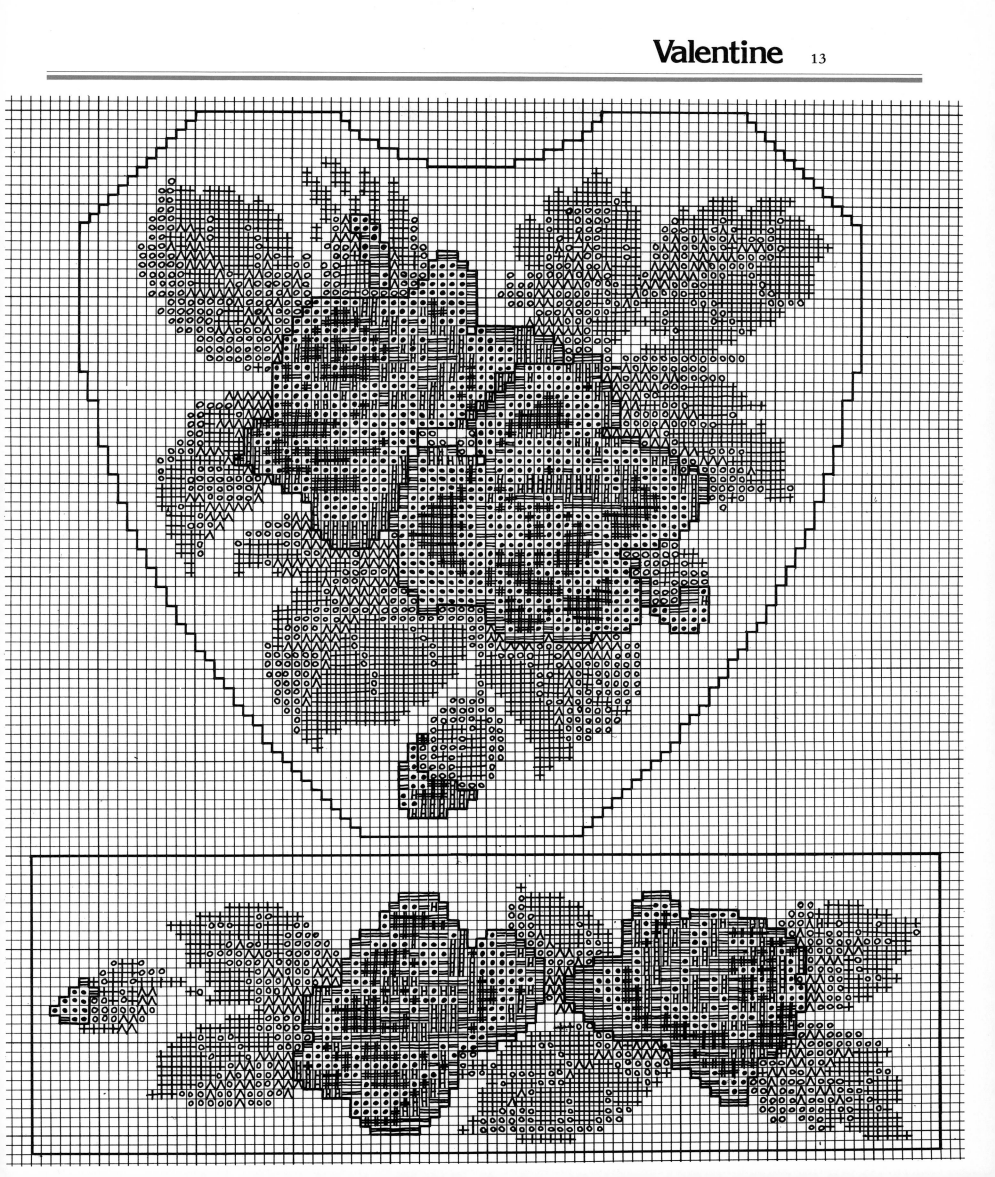

Increase design 15% before tracing onto #10 needlepoint canvas.

For graph of train car, see page 70.

A

B

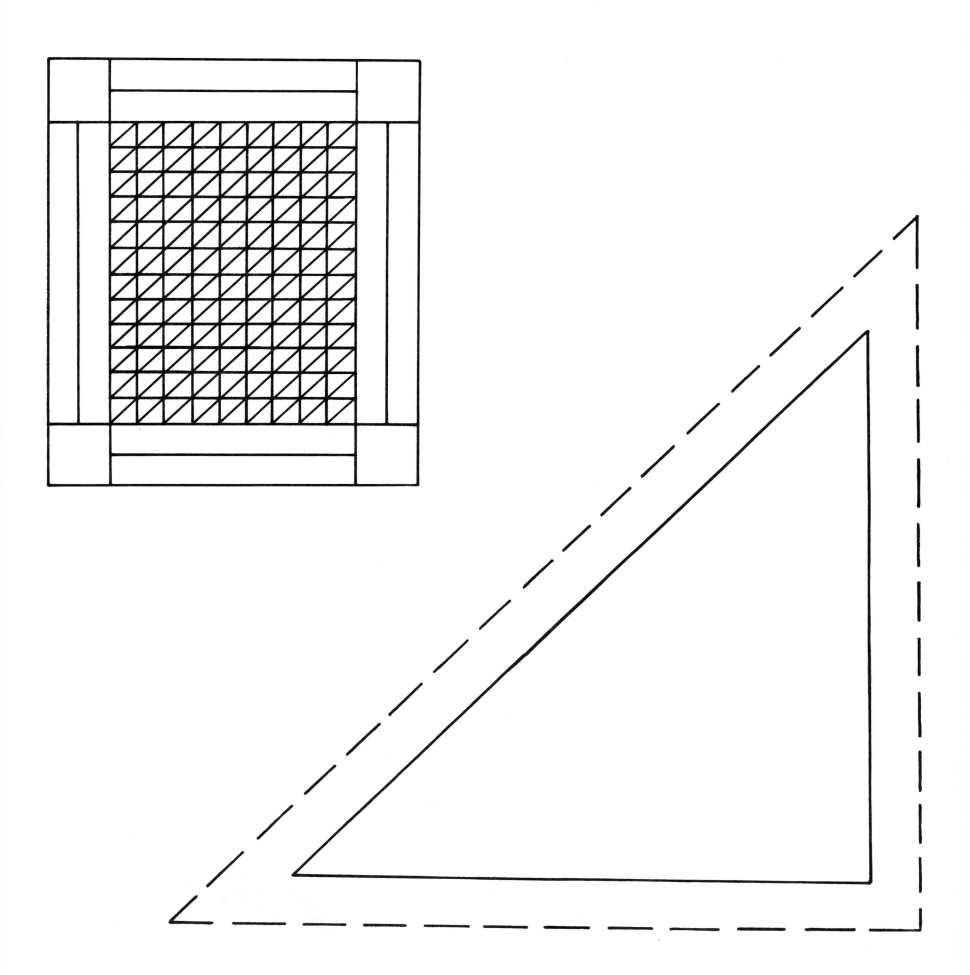

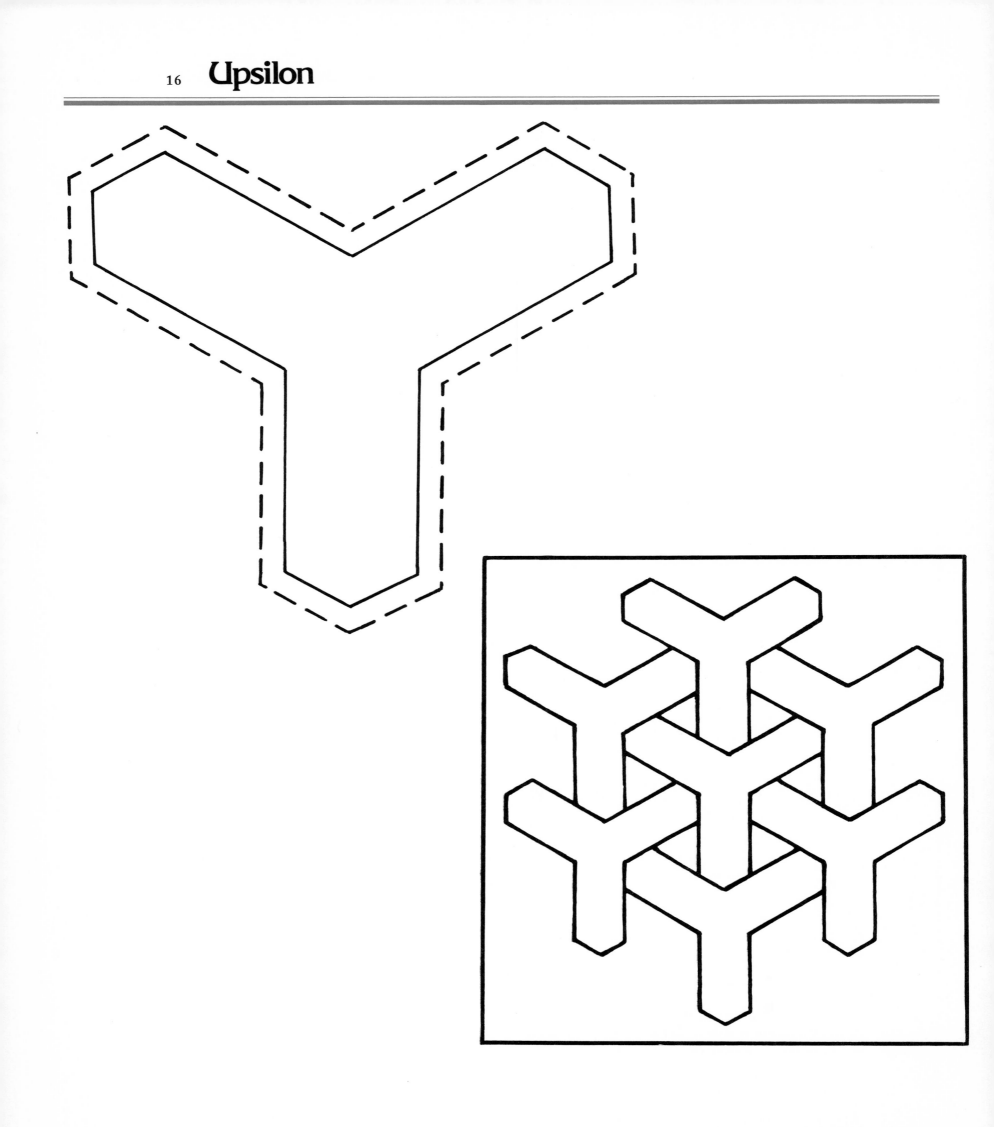

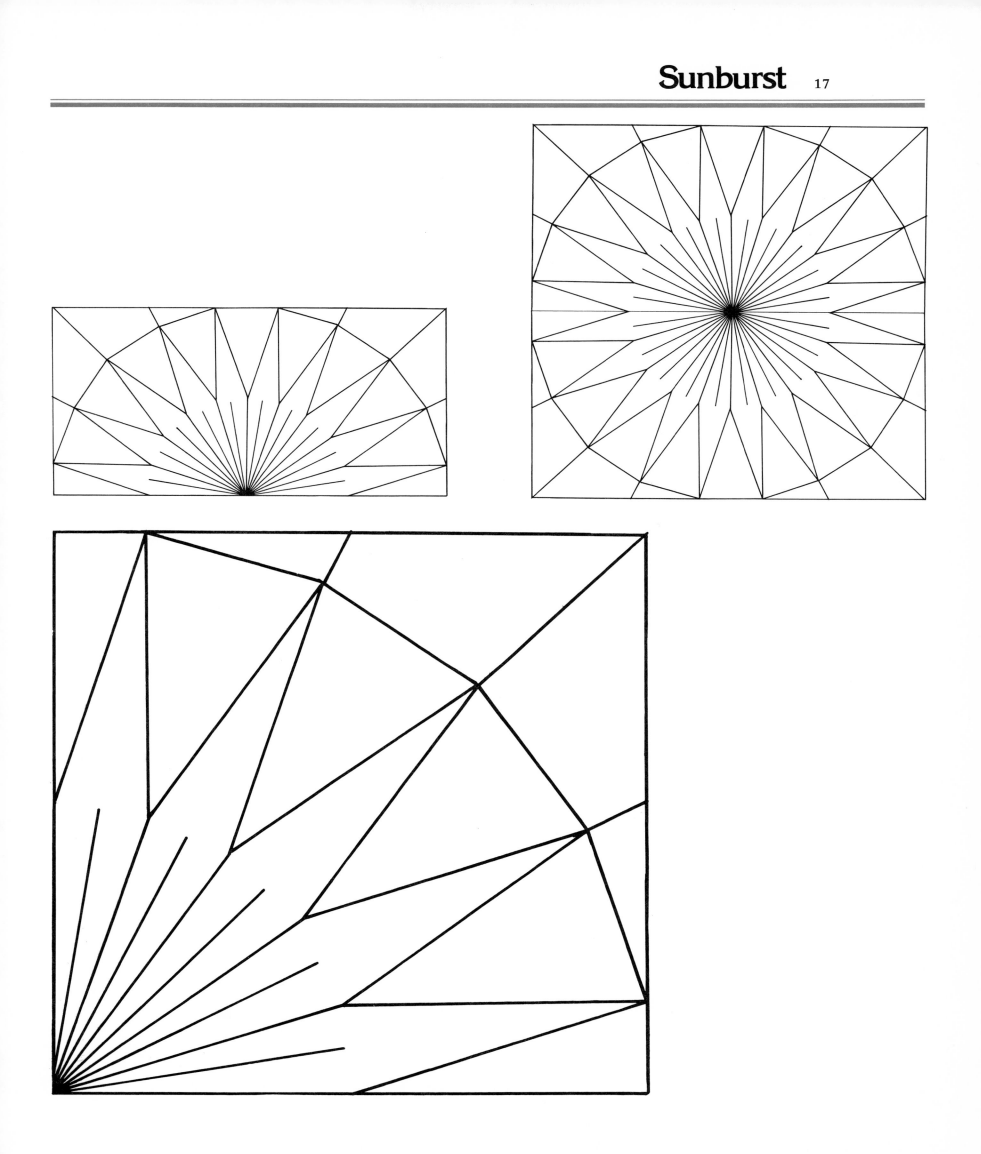

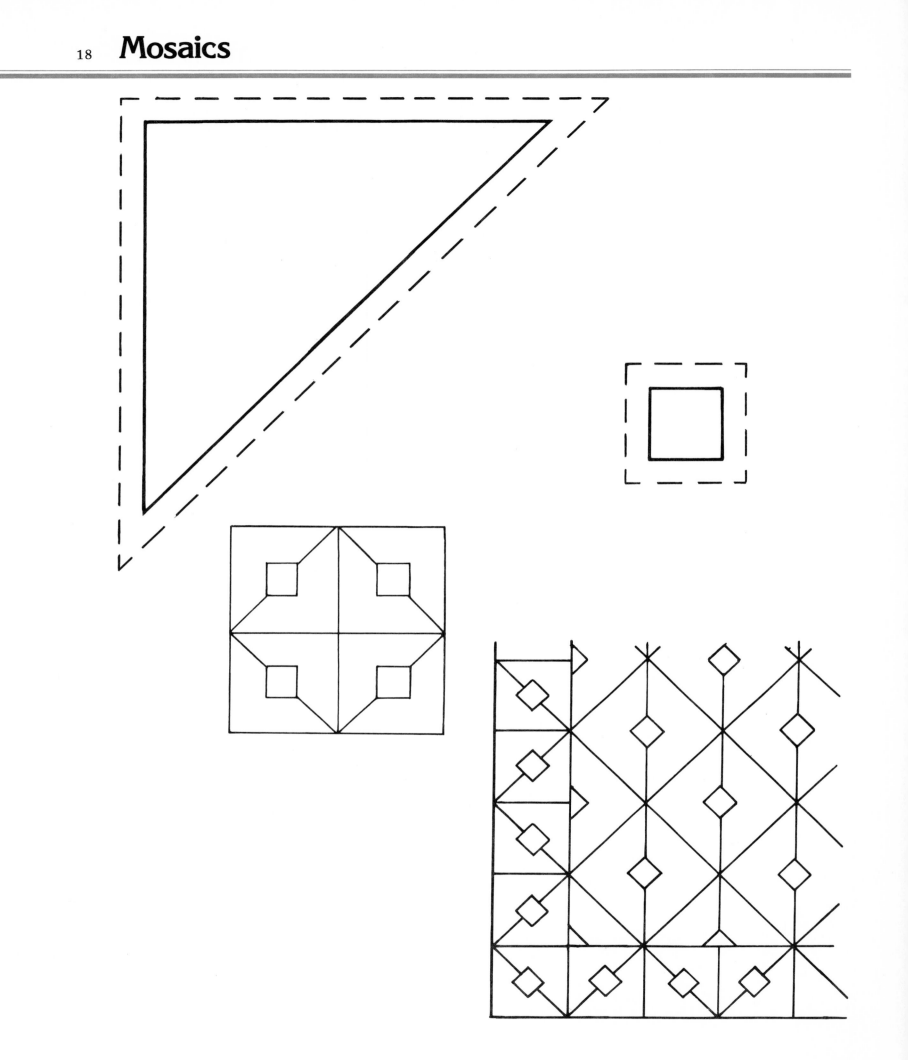

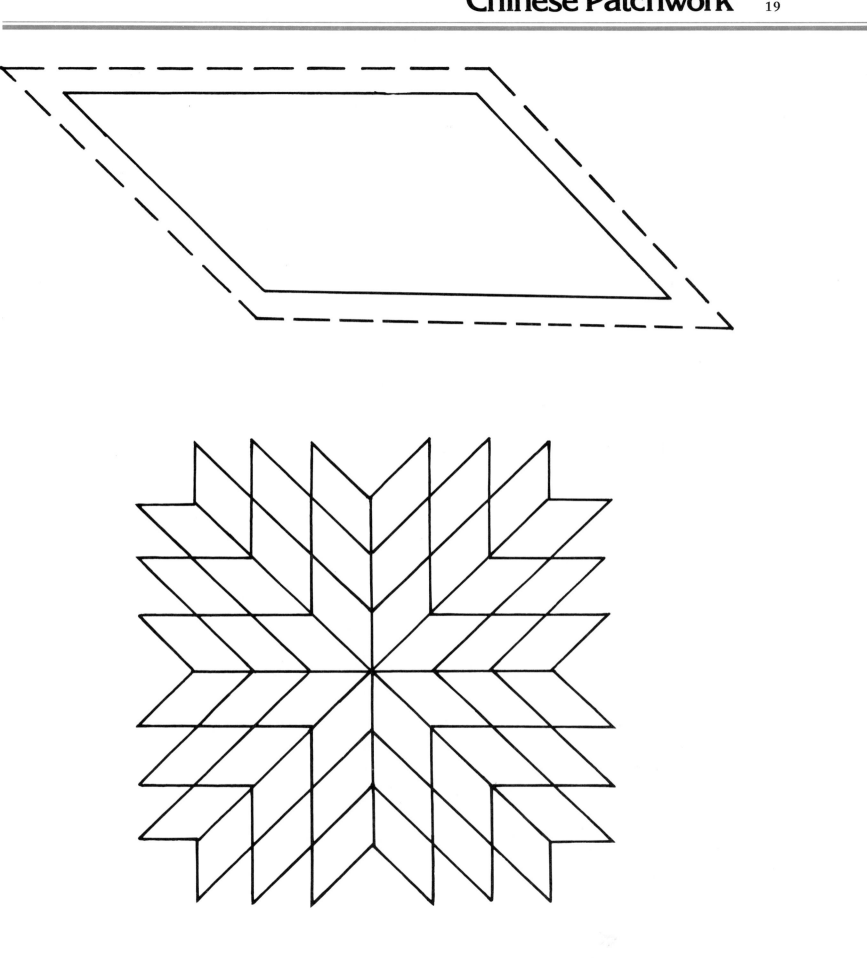

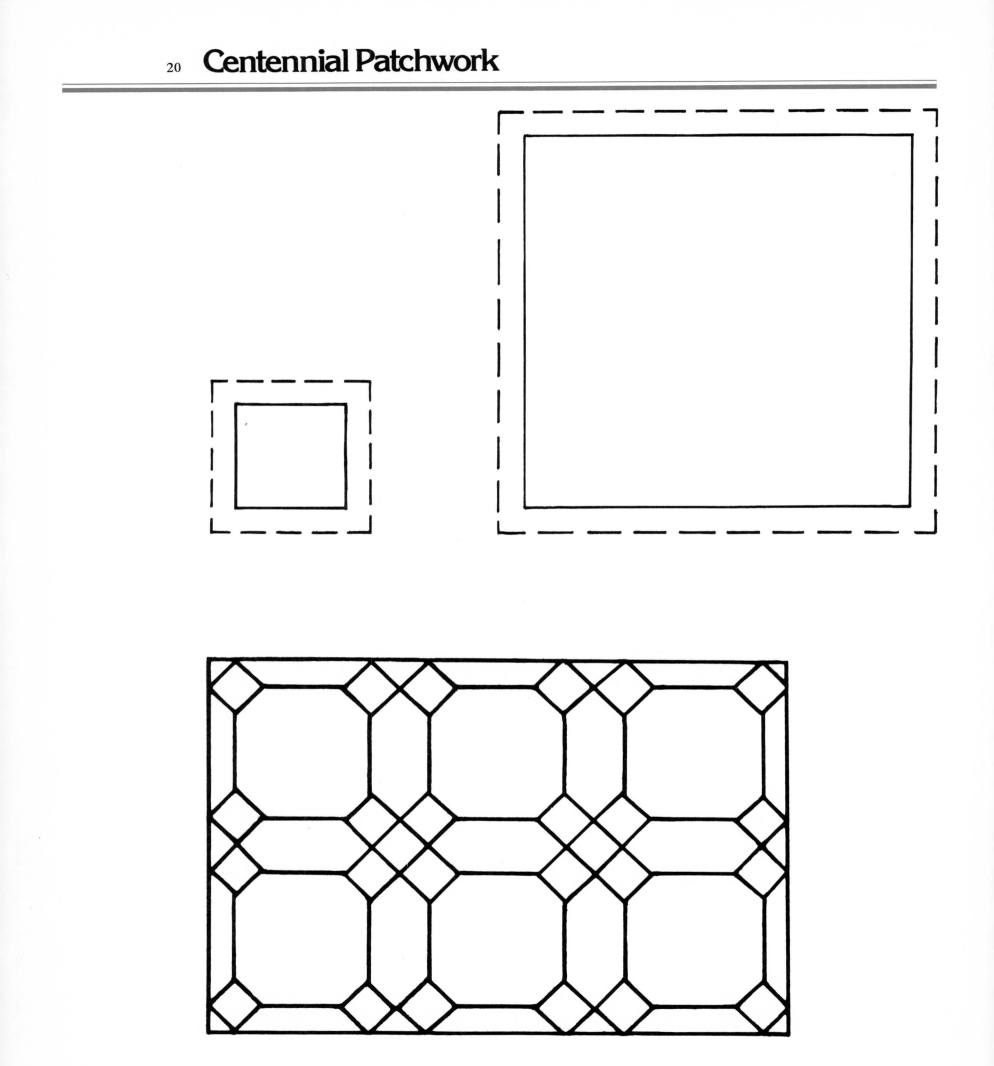

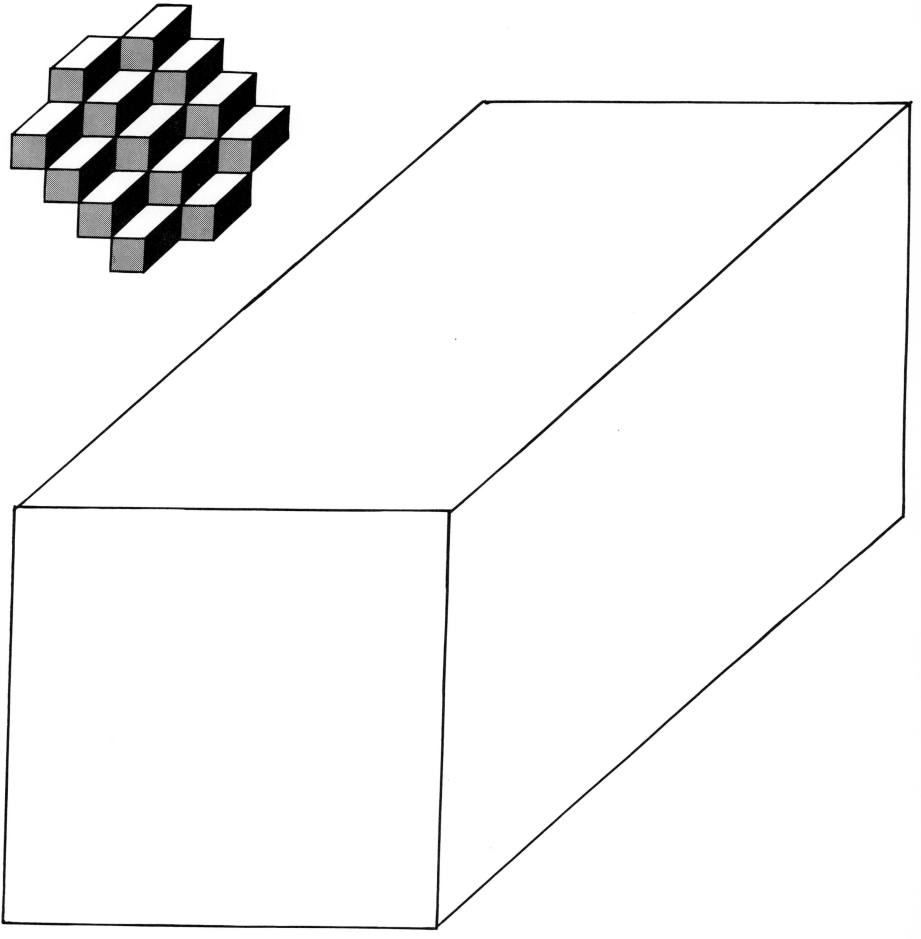

FLORALS

TIMELESS ROSES, *design plate, page 25.*

"This exquisite affair is a design for a chair seat . . . and is printed here in no less than thirteen colors." So wrote the editor of *Peterson's* in January, 1863. She went on to write that this especially lovely design, " . . . is the most costly embellishment *of any kind* we·have ever published. At any trimming store in New York or Philadelphia, this pattern or a similar one would sell for a dollar. Yet we furnish it, besides all the other engravings, illustrations, and reading matter in this number, for only 18¢. The outlay required to get out this one embellishment would buy a handsome farm, buildings and all, in any rural district."

The size given in color on the design plate is appropriate for petit point on #20 canvas and would be especially beautiful as a footstool cushion or framed for hanging. It should be enlarged to work in needlepoint on #10 canvas.

DAISY SPRAY, *design plate, page 26; photo, page 23.*

The daisy is a traditional American design suggesting the outdoors and the summer sun. It has appeared in American needlework designs from the time of the American Revolution. Other flowers like pink chrysanthemums, blue asters, or black-eyed Susans are so similar that their colors could be substituted for those of a daisy. The rendition of this design in crewel-work for a corner of the "Flower Patch Quilt" shown on page 23 suggests a bouquet of asters and chrysanthemums in pinks and blues.

Incredible as it may seem, in 1887 when this design was first published in *The Delineator* "the construction and decoration of tennis-racquet covers [supplied] pretty and interesting occupation to ladies who play or whose friends enjoy the game." Enlarge this design and work in needlepoint for one side of a tennis racquet cover and to make it truly authentic, needlepoint your initials (use one of the alphabets illustrated in this book) in a pleasing combination for the reverse side.

FIELD POPPIES, *design plate, page 27; photo, page 23.*

A spray of red field poppies on black satin was suggested as a design for a scarf or work-bag in 1889. It is especially appropriate in crewel work for a corner of the "Flower Patch Quilt" in color on page 23. Or, enlarge it for the central motif on a needlepoint pillow. If you're a Californian, do your translation in the bright yellow of the California Poppy, the State flower.

WILD NARCISSI, *design plate, page 28.*

The flower is the Poet's Narcissus. This design appeared in *Peterson's* in October, 1889, apparently so that one might stitch away the winter evenings with the thought constantly present of the fragrant flowers that would appear in early Spring. Although originally designed for an embroidered chair back, "Wild Narcissi" would be especially beautiful as a pillow or picture in needlepoint or embroidery.

MORNING GLORIES, *design plate, page 29; photo, page 6.*

This Art Nouveau design for a cushion first appeared in an 1890 magazine. The heart-shaped green leaves offset the trumpet-shaped flowers which may be blue, purple, red, pink, or white to suit your fancy. *Peterson's* needlework editor suggested painting the flowers on the fabric and then outlining the shapes with embroidery in rope-silk or linen. An especially appropriate design for needlepoint or petit point, this intricate design presents a challenge to the experienced needleworker. Use it as a pillow-top or frame it as a picture like ours.

FLORAL SCROLL, *design plate, page 32; photo, page 23.*

This 1916 design was originally a stamping pattern for embroidery on the bodice of a dress. It was enlarged for a corner of the "Flower Patch Quilt" (page 23) and worked in satin stitch, French knots, lazy daisy, and outline stitch with wool crewel yarns.

1. Flower Patch Quilt, page 15.
2. Floral Scroll, page 30.
3. Daisy Spray, page 26.
4. Nosegay, Page 51.
5. Field Poppies, page 27.

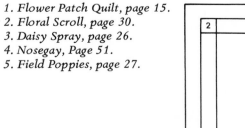

NOSEGAY, *design plate, page 31; photo, page 23.*

This design was available in 1911 as a Butterick needlework stamping pattern for a 3″ border to embroider on the overskirt of a dress. It was enlarged and adapted for a corner of "Flower Patch Quilt" (page 23) and worked in crewel yarns. The central flower and one spray would be beautiful, too, repeated around the bottom of a long velveteen hostess skirt worked in quilting stitches or trapunto (see page 90).

ORIENTAL MEDALLION, *design plate, page 32; photo, page 11.*

Oriental dressing gowns were very fashionable during the Art Déco period. This floral medallion appeared originally as a pattern for "painting, appliqué, quilting, or stenciling" on just such a gown. We found it especially suited to shadow quilting (page 90) using white cotton dotted Swiss over gold cotton broadcloth. After the quilting is completed on a 13″ circle add two rows of ruffled eyelet as shown and complete the pillow (page 91).

DÉCO TULIPS, *design plate, page 33.*

The tulip has blossomed as a design for needlework for many years and it is believed that Dutch settlers brought this flower to America. It appears here in an Art Déco translation which originally appeared in 1928 in the pages of *The Delineator* as a stencil pattern "to brighten dark bits of furniture to make your house young." Use the pattern for appliqué or embroidery on a round cushion or as a design for trapunto or quilting in the squares of a quilt.

TULIP GARDEN, *design plate, page 34; photo, page 67.*

During the 1920's and 30's, as now, patchwork experienced a revival. It became the favorite pastime of many, including Marion Davies, a popular star of the silent screen. This bright little patchwork design was available in pattern form in 1930. Although Art Déco in feeling, it is an old "early American" patchwork design. Our version as a 14″ pillow was done in little calico prints in a combination of patchwork and appliqué. Piece all background shapes together, then appliqué tulip and diagonal strips at each corner by hand or by machine with satin stitch. This design could also be interpreted in needlepoint for coasters, greeting cards, or pillows.

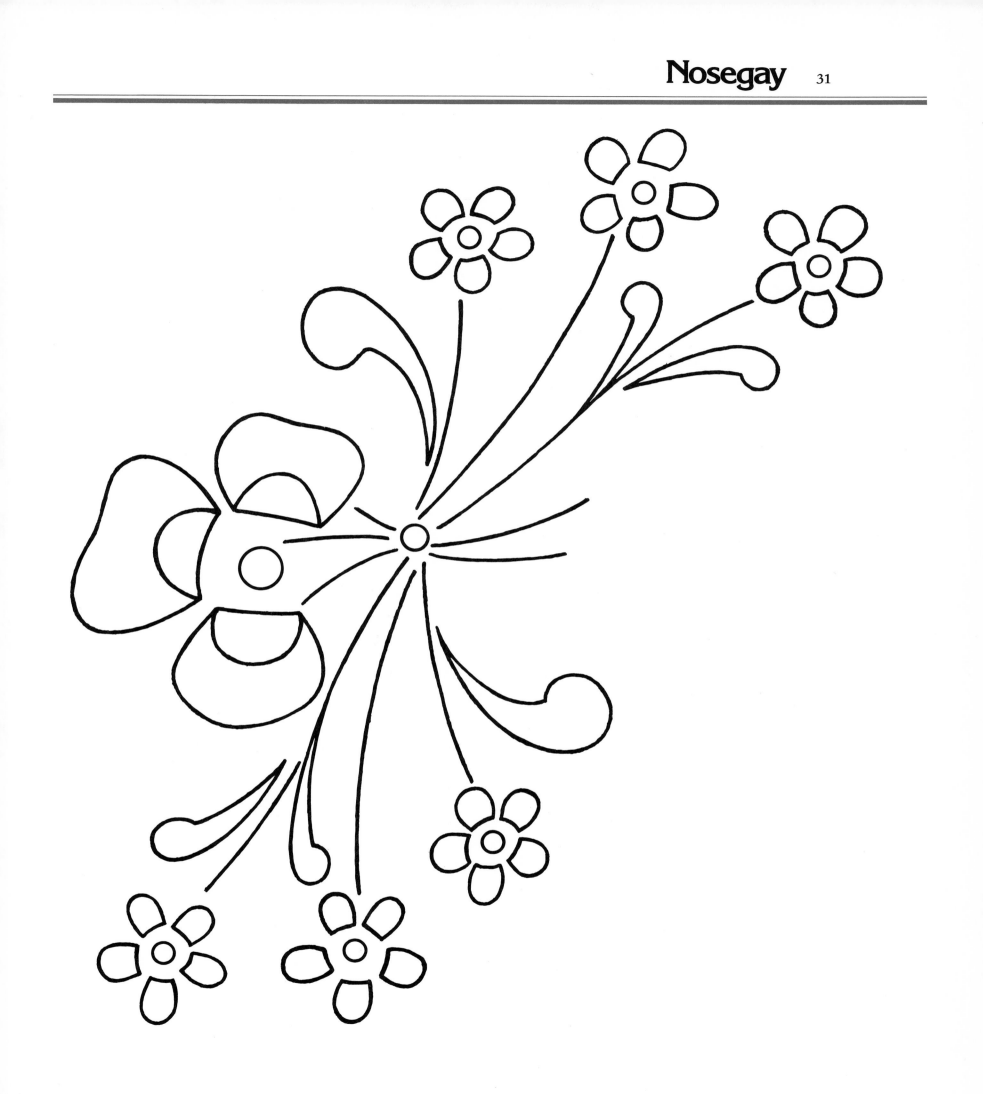

Tulip Garden

ANIMALS

FEATHERED FRIENDS, *design plate, page 37; photo, page 36.*

The original design for these ducks and chick comes from a 1910 edition of *Butterick Designs,* a home catalog of transfer patterns. Our "Feathered Friends" were sketched in carefully fractured segments like a jigsaw puzzle. They were designed as a stencil pattern for the curtains and coverlet of a child's room.

The current translation is an especially contemporary example of appliqué in dotted Swiss and gingham on cotton sailcloth. Tiny details were done in satin stitch embroidery (see page 79) and the completed work finished as a pillow for a favorite child.

BUTTERFLY JEWEL, *design plate, page 38; photo, page 62.*

The brightly colored, jewel-like wings of the butterfly are a perennial favorite interpreted in countless ways with needle and thread. This 1913 design from an early Butterick publication was originally intended for white embroidery on the collar of a white blouse. The pattern is given in two sizes, the smaller appropriate for a framed miniature done in crewel or silk embroidery, the larger for an appliqué or needlepoint picture. Or, capture the gossamer quality of its wings on a pillow top. Appliqué the larger butterfly in layers of sheer organza or chiffon with satin accents and details added in silk embroidery.

CHANTICLEER, *design plate, page 39.*

Our colorful "Chanticleer" for appliqué in bright scraps of satin and silk highlighted with embroidery stitches would "rule the roost" as a wall hanging in your breakfast nook. Also suitable for needlepoint or embroidery, work this sassy barnyard king in a combination of wool, silk, and velvet yarns for picture or pillow. This 1911 design is living proof that good design is timeless.

DINNERTIME, *design plate, page 40; photo, page 36.*

In 1924 lucky children found these kittens embroidered on their new Christmas smocks, aprons, or bedspreads. The design is included here in a size suitable for outline embroidery and in a larger size appropriate for an appliquéd pillow top as shown on page 36. Appliqué was done with a fusible bonding material (page 85) and then embellished with embroidery stitches.

BARTHOLOMEW BUNNY, *design plate, page 41; photo, page 67.*

Stuffed cloth toys were a favorite gift for children in the mid-twenties. "Bartholomew Bunny" was one of eight animals included in a *Butterick Transfers* pattern in 1927.

Increase the pattern given on the design plate to 18" high and work Bartholomew in needlepoint on #10 canvas. To make his cottontail big and fluffy, use the Turkey work needlepoint stitch (page 83). Work his pants in checks of four stitches by four stitches or in stripes of color four stitches wide.

EBENEZER ELEPHANT, *design plate, page 42; photo, page 36.*

The largest animal in the world suddenly appears small, round, and warm with a Christmas star shining on his saddle blanket. In 1927, he appeared as an 18" stuffed toy, but he's especially nice in needlepoint for a round pillow or framed for a child's room. Try him, too, in appliqué for pillows or quilt blocks.

CHEVIOTS, *design plate, page 43; photo, pages 36, and 62.*

Butterick Quarterly Magazine was primarily a home catalog of current Butterick patterns for sewing and needlework. But on its pages one can often find delightful illustrations like these sophisticated Art Déco sheep (1928) which we show in needlepoint and in appliqué to illustrate the versatility of almost any design.

The pattern on the design plate shows the placement line for overlapping the sheep in a row and the small drawings are suggestions for other arrangements. For the needlepoint picture on #10 canvas, the Byzantine stitch, Bargello stitch, and slanting Gobelin stitch were used in the bodies of the sheep. Upright Gobelin over four mesh forms the grass. An entirely different effect was achieved with a combination of machine appliqué and embroidery on white dotted Swiss for the pillow on page 36.

SHADOW CAT, *design plate, page 44.*

This elegant Art Déco cat is indicative of the strong Egyptian influence of the period. The cat was sacred to the ancient Egyptians who were the first people known to tame cats and keep them in their homes. "Shadow Cat" appeared as a page illustration in a 1928 issue of *The Delineator.* Work him in needlepoint or appliqué.

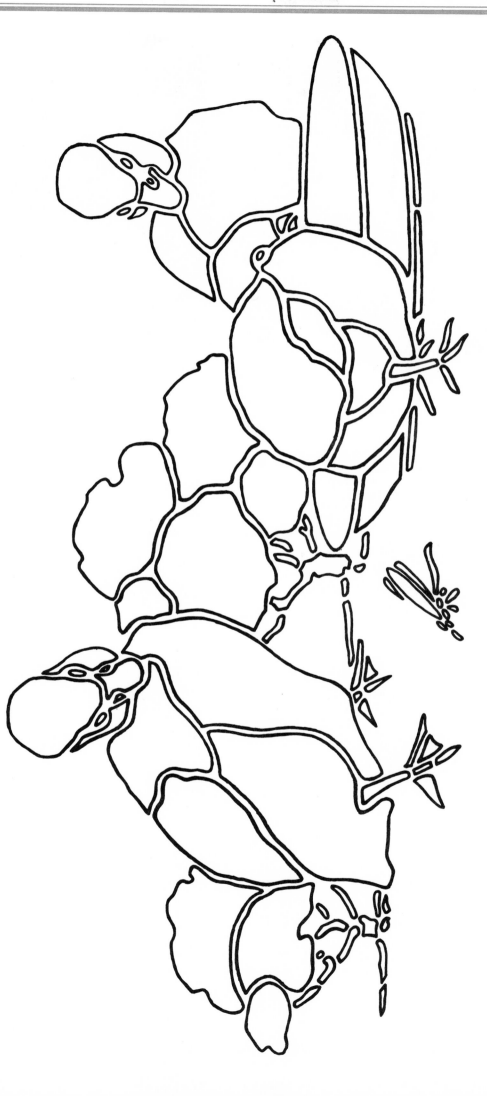

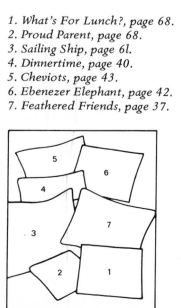

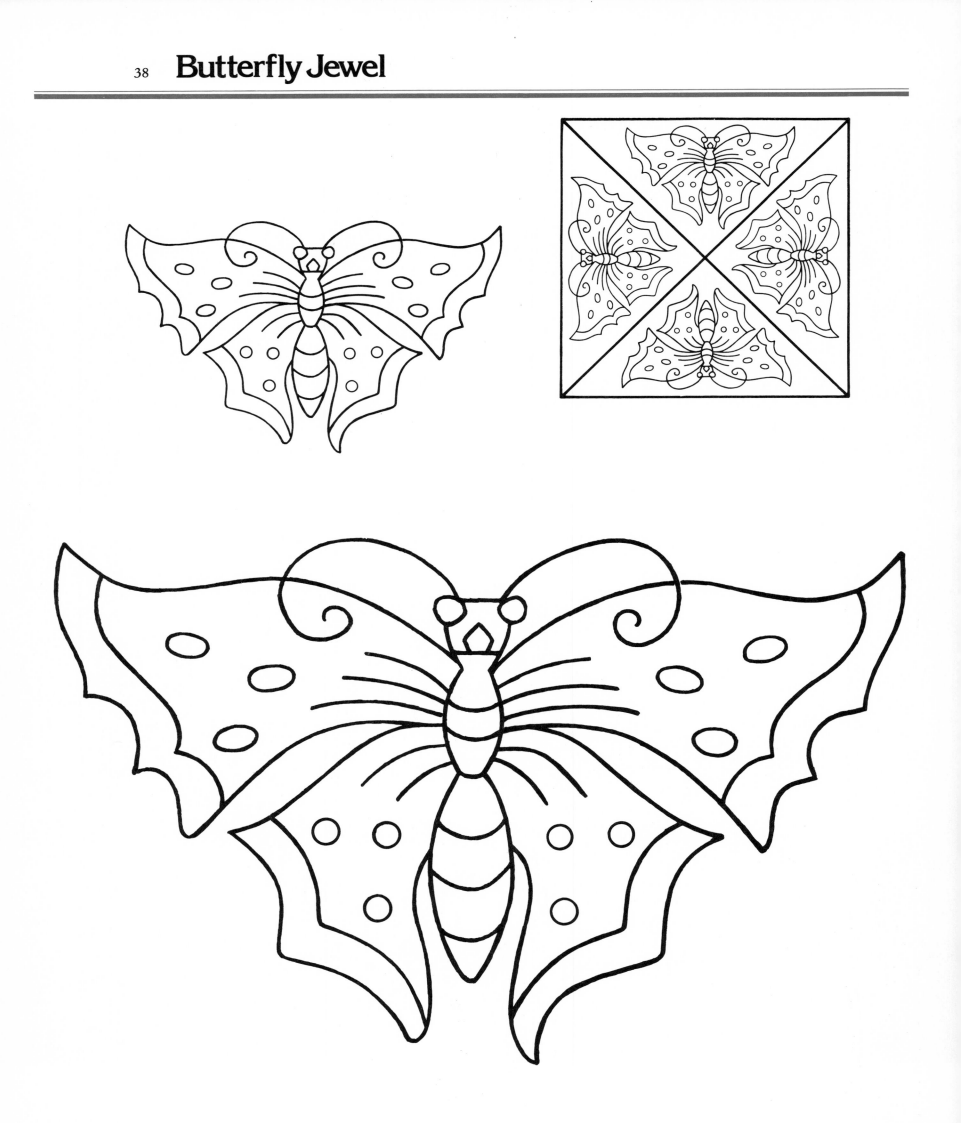

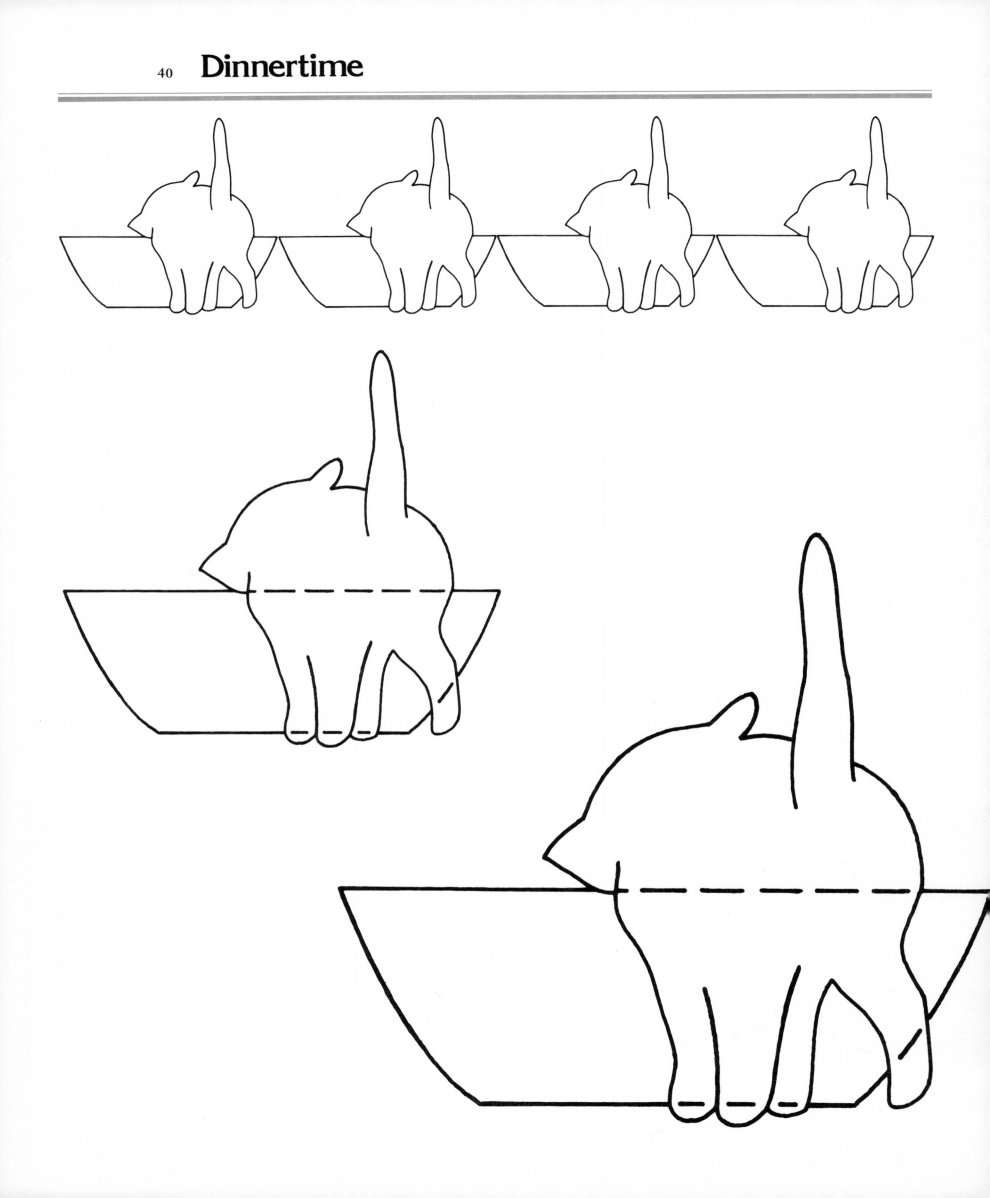

ALPHABETS

Alphabet Collection

The desire to mark one's personal items of clothing and linens with an initial is a tradition of long-standing. It was an occupation of the Victorian age to be sure. In 1893, Butterick published a "pamphlet" of over 100 pages filled with alphabets of every imaginable design "suitable for articles of all dimensions from blankets to doiley's," to be done in "cross-stitch, beading, crochet, embroidery, and painting." The three shown here were taken from *Artistic Alphabets for Marking and Engrossing.*

CROSS-STITCH ALPHABET, *design plate, page 47; photo, page 46.*

Arranged in the squares of a multi-colored patchwork gingham quilt for a special baby, these cross-stitch letters were originally designed for beading. To make the 30″ x 36″ quilt as shown, you will need 1/4 yard of each of five to seven colors of 1/4″ gingham checks and an extra yard and one half (45″ wide) of one of the colors for the quilt backing. Cut a total of thirty 6-1/2″ squares. Cross-stitch a letter in the center of each square with embroidery floss or pearl cotton. Use flower included with alphabet for the corners. Piece completed squares together using 1/2″ seam allowances. Finished piecing should measure 31″ x 37″.

To assemble quilt, cut a rectangle of gingham for quilt backing 44″ wide by 50″ long. Cut a sheet of batting 37″ wide by 43″ and center on top of backing. Center completed quilt top on top of batting and baste all three layers together. Batting should extend 3″ beyond quilt top on all sides. Turn excess backing over batting and onto quilt top. Turn under 1/2″ all around,

mitering corners and slip stitch in place. Tie layers together at the corners of each square using embroidery floss or several strands of pearl cotton (see page 89 for tying instructions).

FLORAL ALPHABET, *design plate, page 50; photo, page 67.*

Embroider this lovely old alphabet in satin stitch and lazy daisy on your favorite napkins and matching placemats or use it on a silk shirt or scarf.

FANCY BLOCK ALPHABET, *design plate, page 48; photo, page 6.*

This especially beautiful design is appropriate for satin stitch in the size shown on the design plate. Or, enlarge it to work in quilting as shown on our blue satin evening bag. To make the bag which measures 9″ x 6″ when completed, you will need 1/2 yard satin, 1/2 yard lining fabric, buttonhole twist and 1-1/4 yards decorative cord in a contrasting color, and polyester fiberfill. Cut two rectangles of satin and one of lining fabric. Each should measure 10″ x 19″. Enlarge letter to 5″ height. Center and trace letter on the bottom third of one piece of satin. Form quilting layers with lining on bottom, fiberfill next, and satin with traced letter on top. Baste. Quilt letter by hand with buttonhole twist. With right sides together, stitch quilted piece to remaining satin rectangle in 1/2″ seams leaving a four inch opening. Trim seams and turn bag right side out. Slip stitch opening. Turn one-third of bag up to form pouch and slip stitch edges together securely. Stitch cord onto edges with couching stitch (page 78).

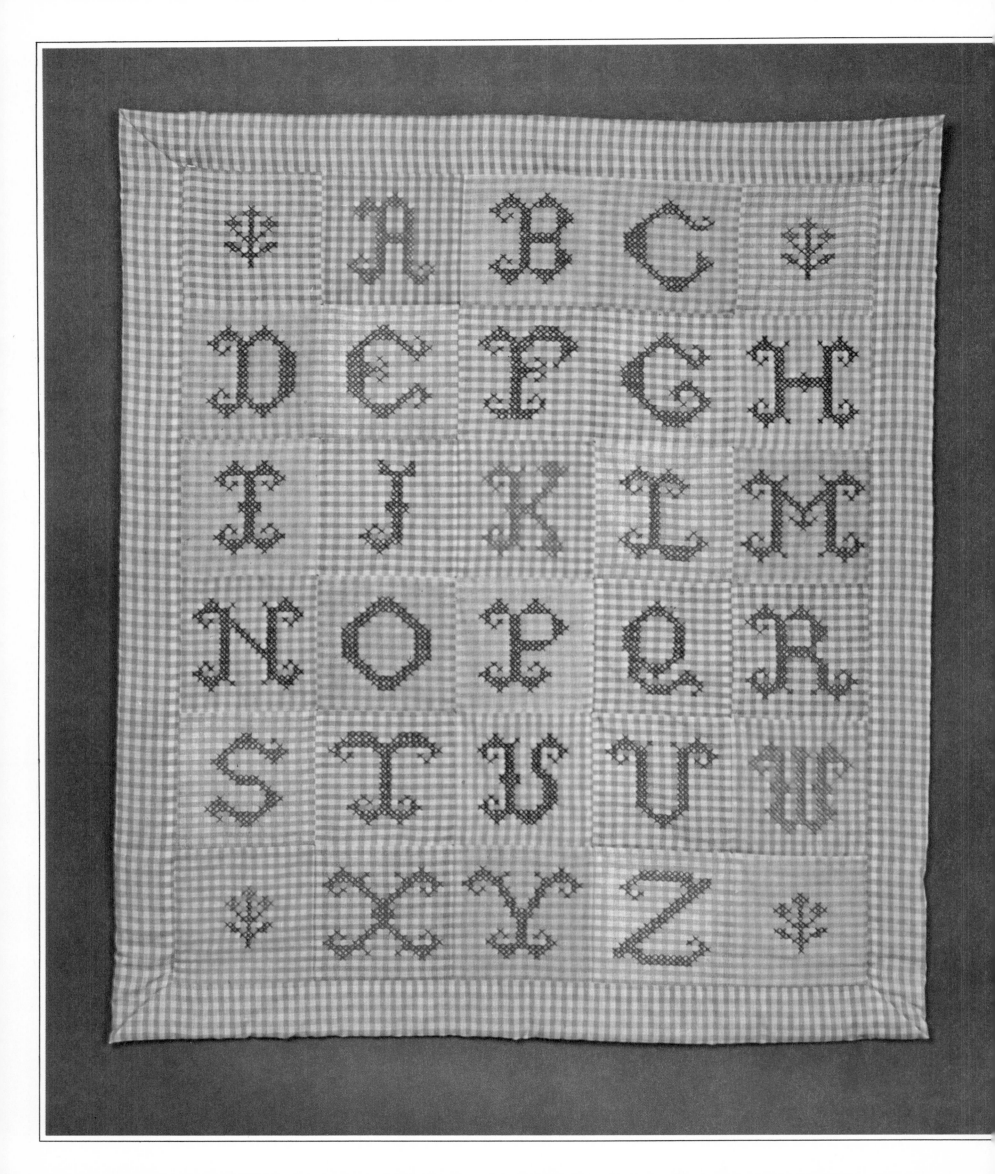

Cross-Stitch Alphabet Quilt, above.

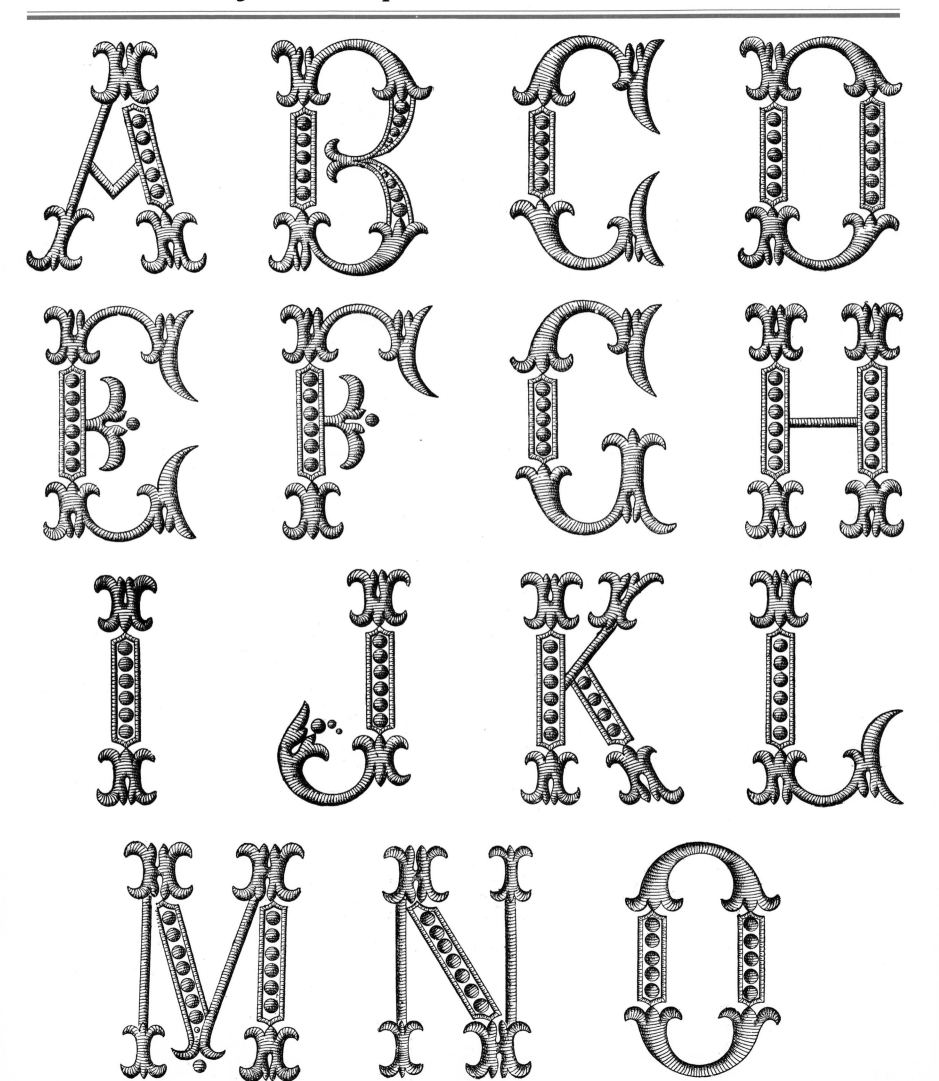

Floral Alphabet

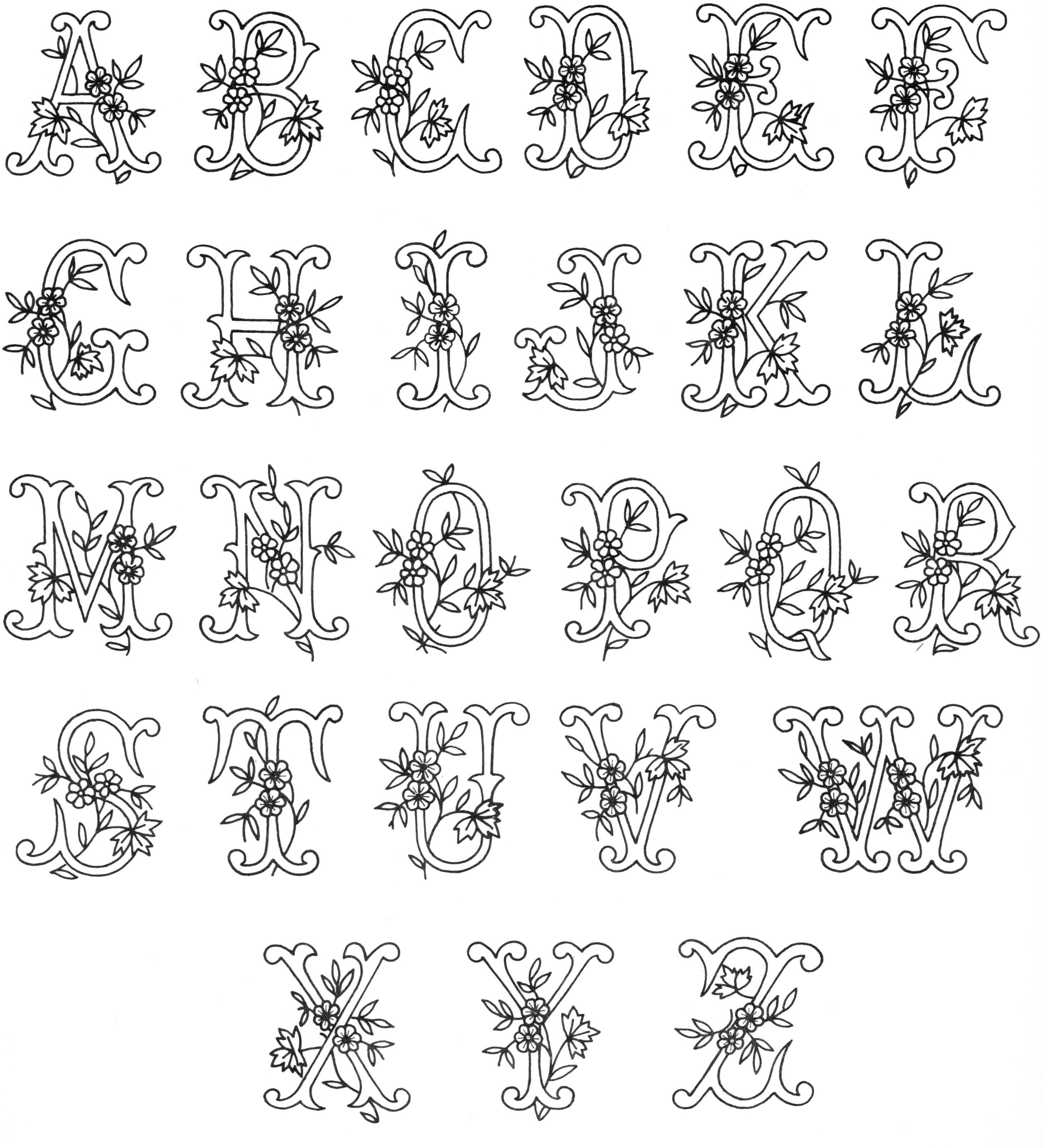

ART DÉCO

HIGH HATTERS, *design plates, pages 52, 53, 54, and 55; photo, page 6.*

The Delineator included the latest news in accessories as a regular feature with its illustrations of current dress patterns. Three of our "High Hatters" were drawings in just such an article. In April, 1925, the "Spring Mode in New Millinery" boasted pompons, roses, water lilies and violets. Popular colors of the period included fuschia, purple, green, powder blue, hydrangea pinks and blues, rose and pastels. The pair of needlepoint pictures illustrated in color on page 6 was worked in some of these same shades. To duplicate the pictures on #10 canvas, use the design plates on pages 52 and 53. Add a border of twelve stitches all around incorporating "Circles and Squares," the "Martha Washington Rose," and "1925" (page 72) as shown in the color photography.

Another "High Hatter," from a 1923 illustration appears as a 14″ round pillow worked in a contemporary appliqué technique known as "fabric collage." Using basic appliqué techniques, a scrap of silk for the dress, apricot chiffon for the face, lace trim for the hat, a strand of pearls, flower buttons, and a ribbon tied in a bow, plus satin stitch embroidery for the lip were combined to create a three-dimensional effect outlined with two rows of ruffled lace (approximately two yards).

TANGO, *design plate, page 56, photo, page 6.*
MOTORING, *design plate, page 57.*
SIESTA, *design plate, page 58.*

The Summer, 1914 issue of *Butterick Designs* was beautifully illustrated with several vignettes including these three. We have adapted them for needlepoint pictures to challenge the experienced needleworker. The intricacy of these designs requires that they be worked in petit point (#20 canvas).

"Tango" was stitched with six shades of embroidery floss in a variation of petit point that produces a slightly ribbed effect on the surface of the finished work. To execute this technique, work on #10 Penelope canvas (see page 81) and split the vertical meshes in each horizontal row. In effect, this means working twenty stitches per inch horizontally and ten stitches per inch vertically which produces a long slanted stitch. Experi-

ment with this stitch on a scrap of canvas before beginning the design.

DÉCO-DIAMOND, *design plate, page 59.*
DÉCO-RAYS, *design plate, page 60; photo, page 62.*

In 1928, the backs of "Congress Playing Cards" boasted these two bold designs, excellent examples of the Art Déco style. They are a challenge for the experienced needlepointer and in the size shown should be worked in petit point. Better still, enlarge them to wall hanging or rug size and appliqué them in brightly colored felt. (See appliqué instructions, page 85.)

SAILING SHIP, *design plate, page 61; photo, page 36.*

Perfectly arranged for a block in a patchwork quilt, "Sailing Ship" was a 1928 design for Armstrong linoleum tile as advertised in the pages of *The Delineator*. Work it in needlepoint in shades of blue on a white ground or try it in a combination of appliqué and shadow quilting (page 90).

To duplicate our pillow, cut a 19″ square of each of the following: white silk organza, white cotton broadcloth, and red on white dotted Swiss. Center and draw a 12″ square on the broadcloth. Center over design plate and trace. Cut colored rectangles from felt and fuse in place (see page 86). Baste organza square over completed appliqué and stitch around each rectangle. Using buttonhole twist, machine stitch ship outlines (see photo). With right sides together, stitch pillow top to backing (1/2″ seam allowances) leaving one side open. Trim seams, turn and press. Stitch through all layers on lines of 12″ square leaving one side unstitched. Stuff with 12′ pillow form, complete stitching, and slip stitch edge of pillow closed.

BALLOONS, *design plate, page 63; photo, page 62.*
GIRL ON A SWING, *design plate, page 64.*

A pretty pair to work in cross-stitch, needlepoint (#10 canvas) or quick point (#5 canvas and rug yarn) for pillows or pictures to delight any child. Both were originally shown in colored cross-stitch plates on the covers of *Needle-Art* magazine in 1925 and 1926.

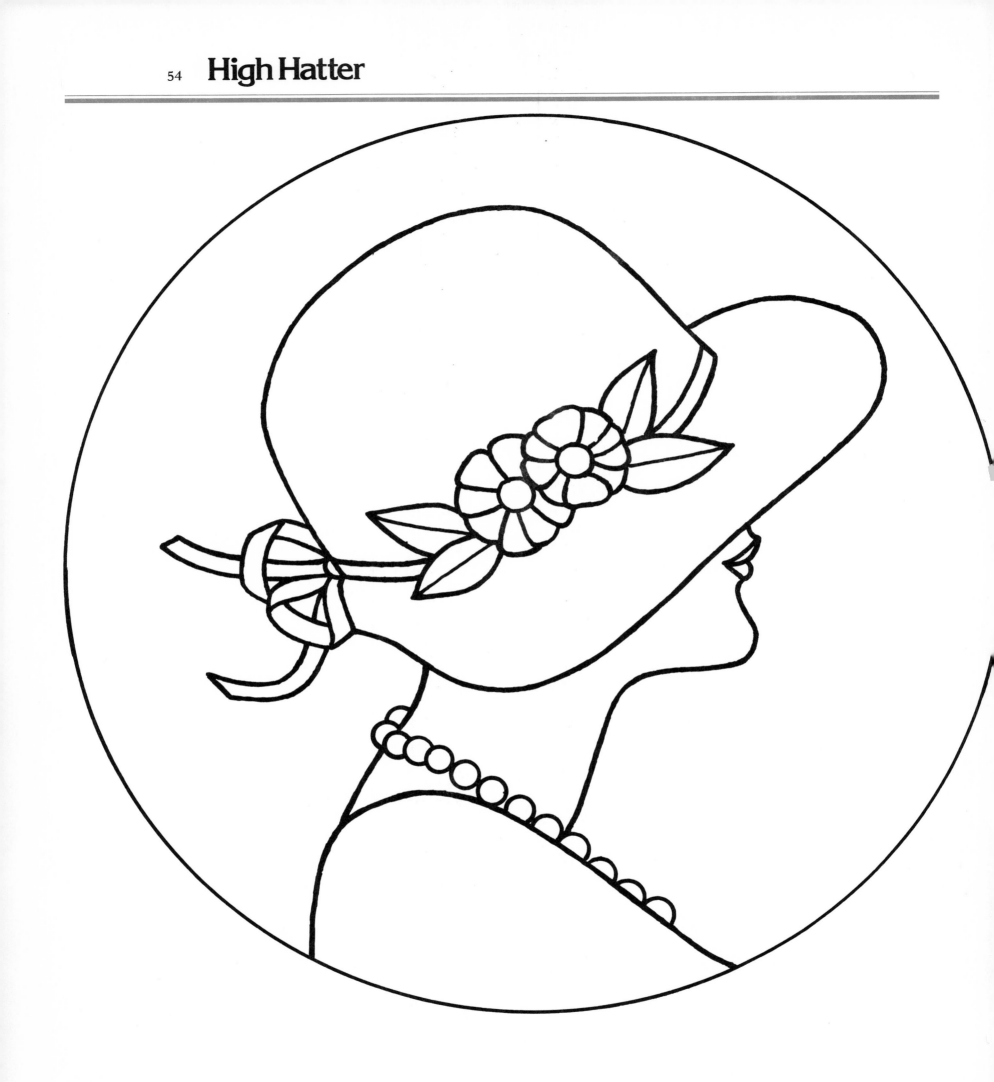

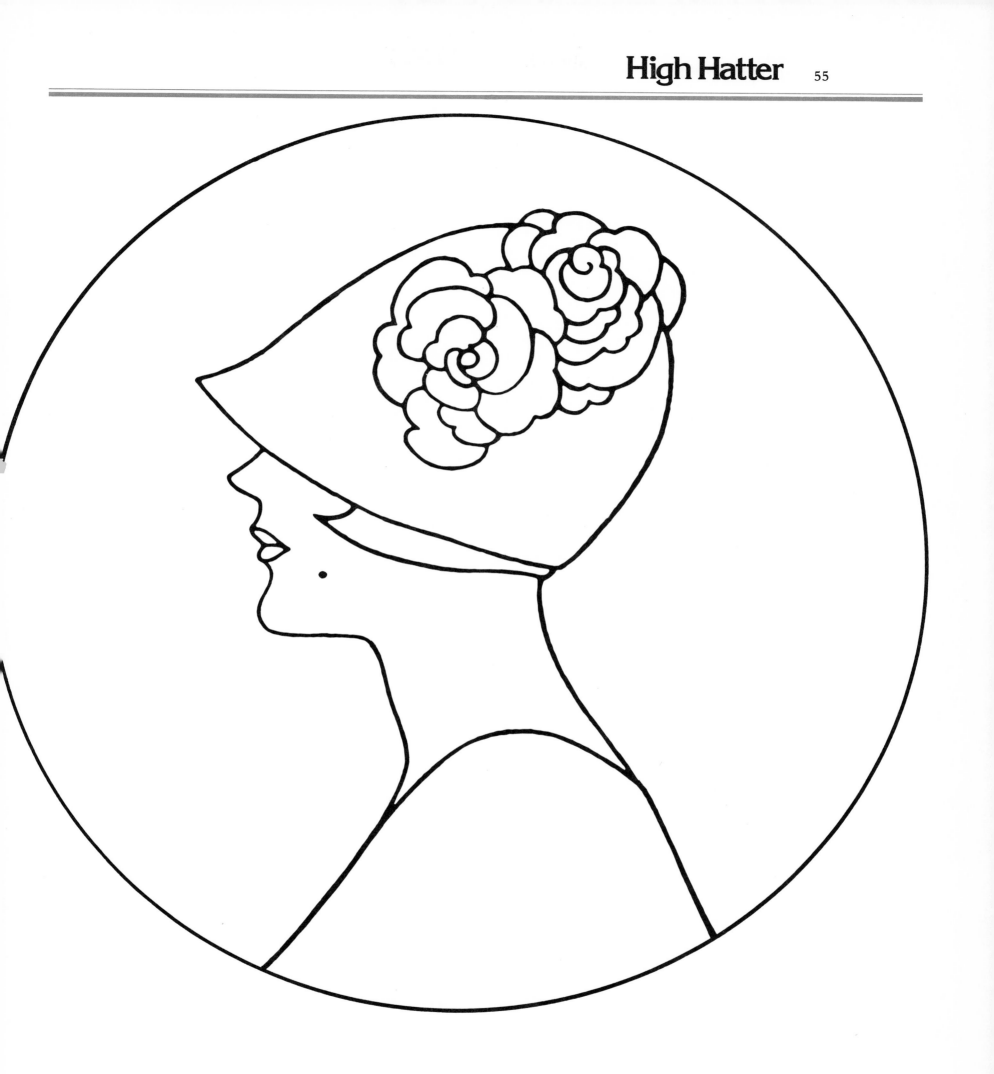

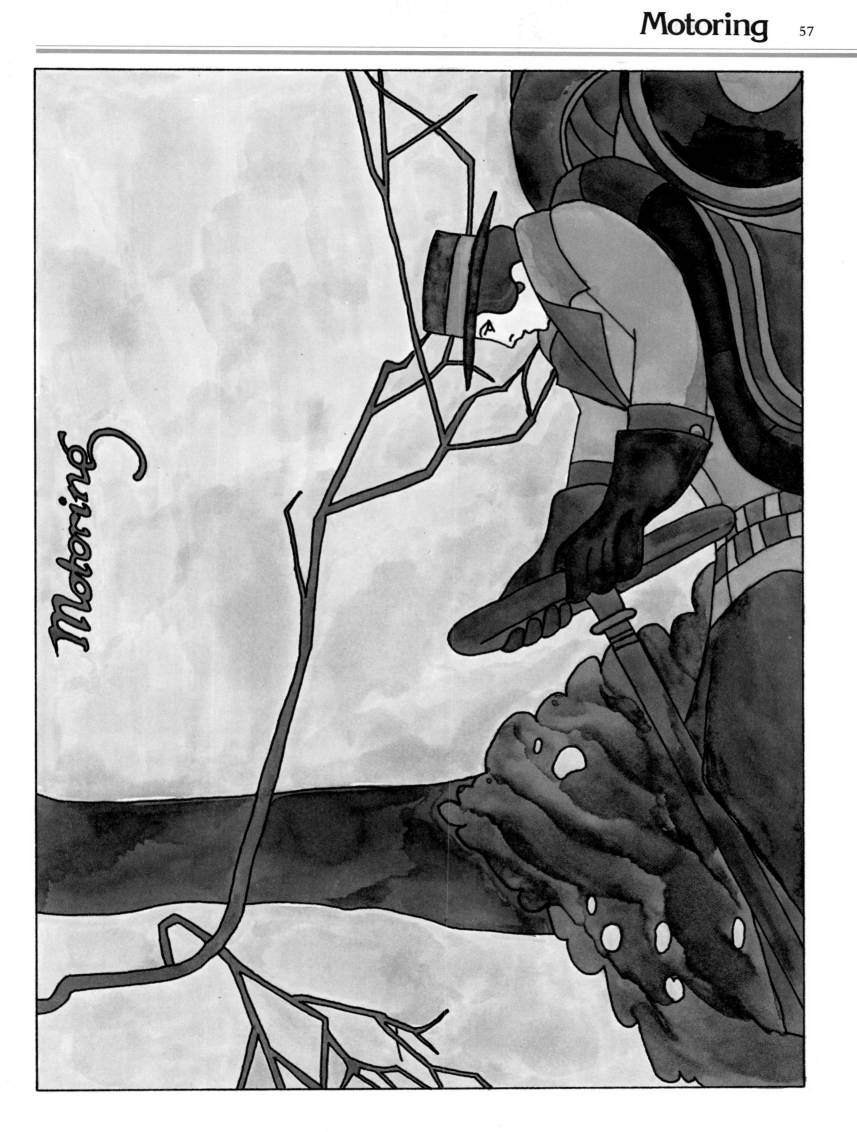

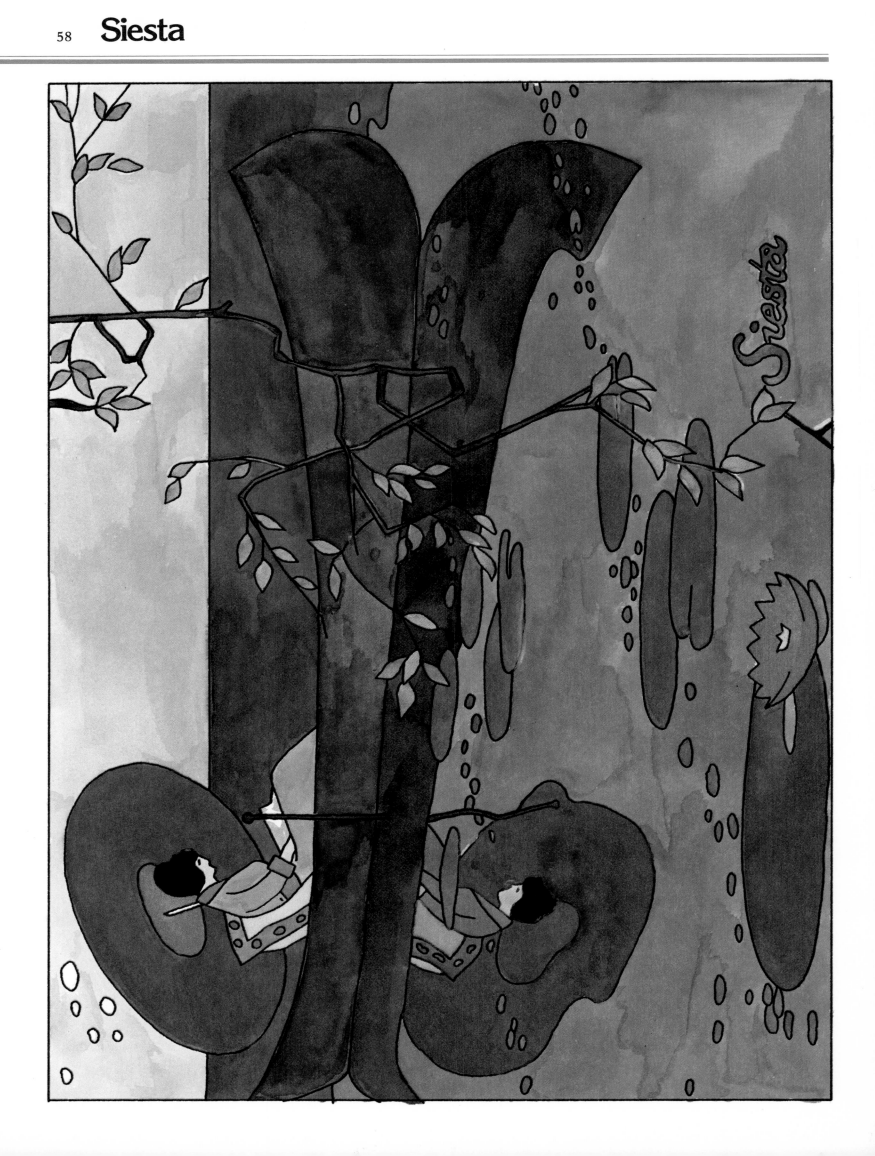

Déco-Rays

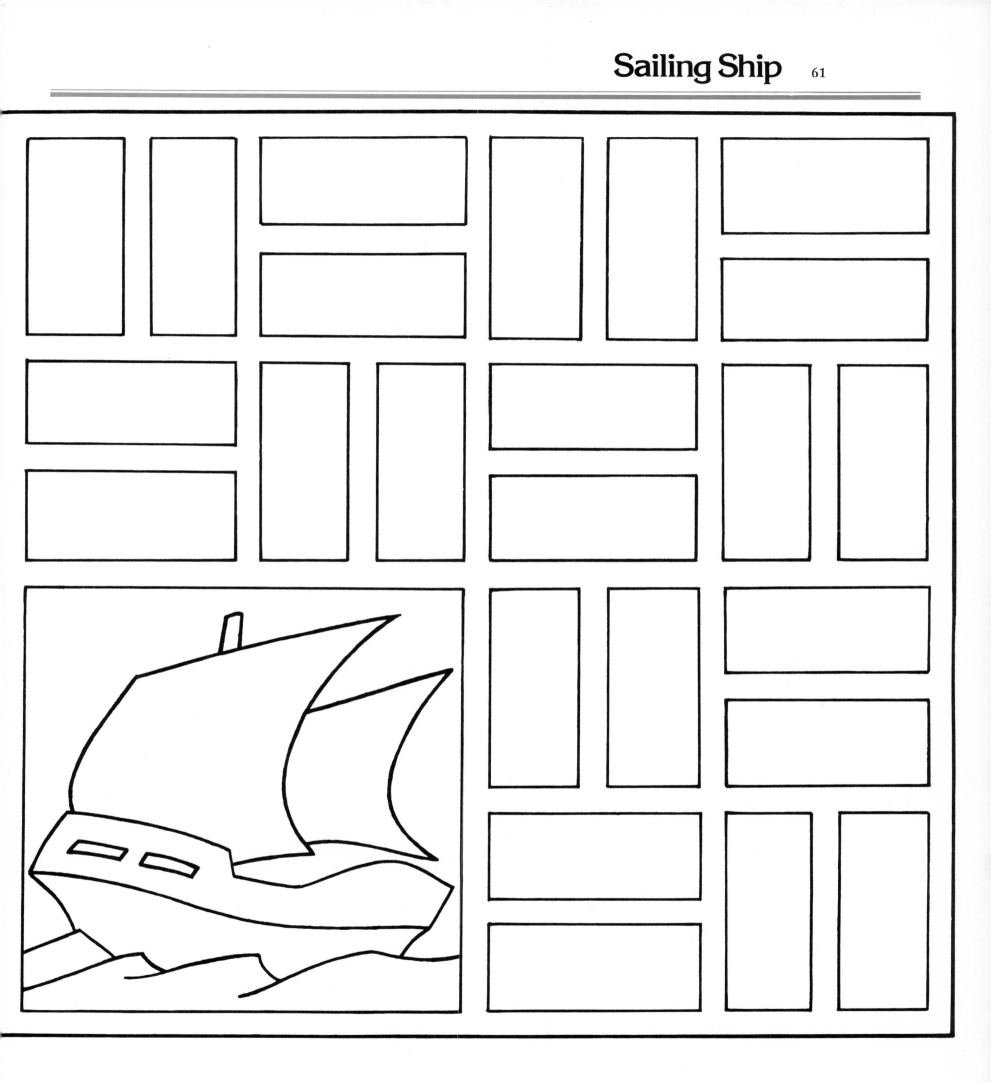

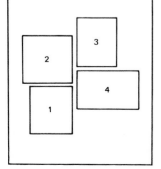

All designs which appear on graphs were done in the scale of 10 stitches per inch. Designs may be worked on any size canvas but size of completed work will change accordingly.

For graph color key, see page 82.

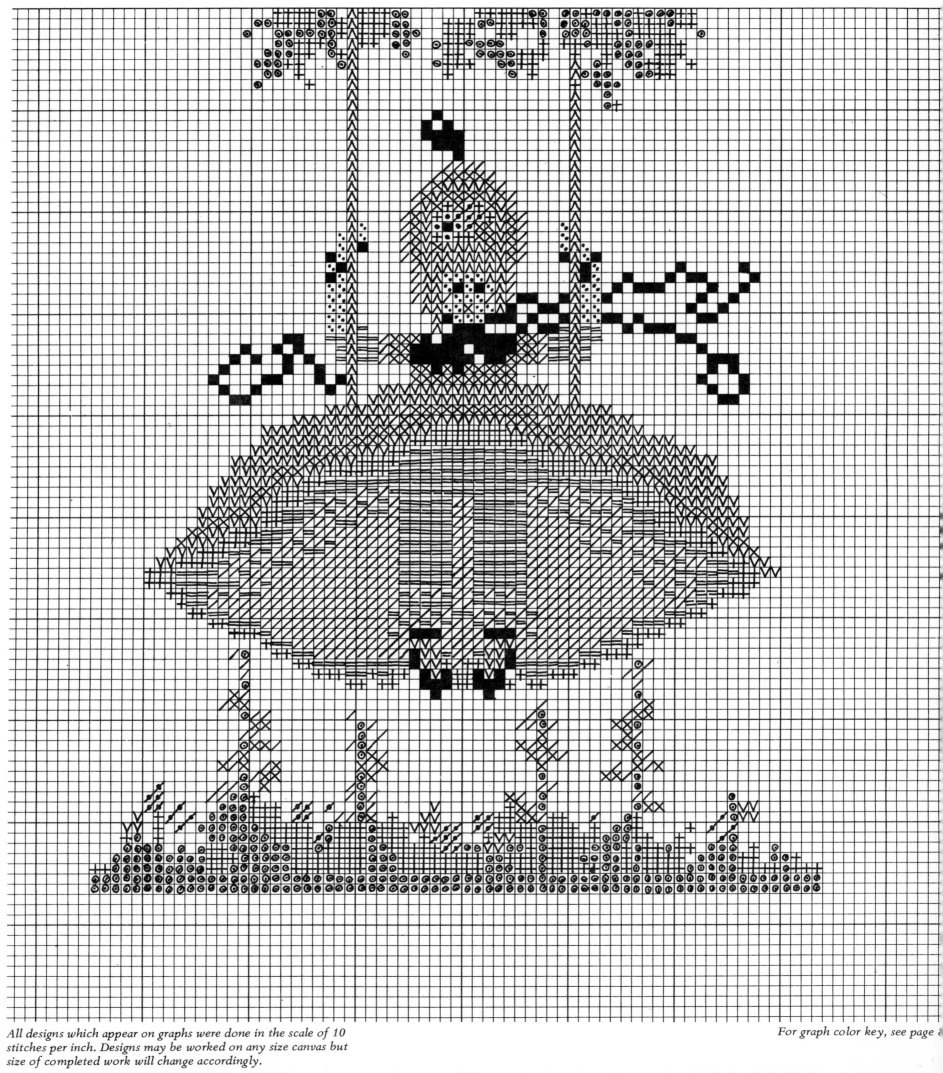

All designs which appear on graphs were done in the scale of 10 stitches per inch. Designs may be worked on any size canvas but size of completed work will change accordingly.

For graph color key, see page

POTPOURRI

WHAT'S FOR LUNCH? *(4″ x 6″), design plate, page 68; photo, page 36.*
PROUD PARENT *(4-1/2″ x 4-1/2″), design plate, page 68; photo, page 36.*

Two delightful designs interpreted as needlepoint pictures for the nursery. They were worked with Persian yarn on #10 canvas, then matted and framed. The mats were made by covering mat board with printed fabric. See page 93 for directions for fabric-covered mats.

NUMERALS, *design plate, page 72.*

Designed for needlepoint or cross-stitch for dating your needlework.

CHRISTMAS BELLS, *design plate, page 70; photo, page 67.*
FRUIT AND FLOWERS, *design plate, page 70; photo, page 67.*

These two pretty borders became watchbands worked in needlepoint. The bands (Wm. E. Wright) can be purchased in a needlework shop or you can make your own by backing the completed needlepoint with a strip of felt or grosgrain ribbon (see page 94) and adding a purchased buckle and eyelets.

FLORAL BORDER AND CORNER, *design plate, page 69.*

A border and corner to use alone or together on a belt, picture frame, or watchband.

PUZZLE, *design plate, page 69.*

This design originally appeared in *Peterson's Magazine* in 1859 as a pattern for braiding. Use it for that very purpose or for satin stitch embroidery. It would be perfect, too, for needlepoint or quilting.

RICK RACK, *design plate, page 72; photo, page 67.*

Needlepoint napkin rings (#10 canvas) are the contemporary adaptation of this 1924 design for cross-stitch. Try it, too, as a border all around a pillow, on a belt, or as a choker necklace. To make napkin rings, cut an 8″ x 3″ piece of #10 canvas. Work design, then follow instructions on page 94 for backing needlepoint. To finish, form into a ring and stitch the two ends together with matching yarn.

MARTHA WASHINGTON ROSE, *design plate, page 72; photo, page 6.*

A crochet pattern depicting Martha Washington appeared in an 1881 issue of *Peterson's Magazine* and this rose was part of the border design. Use it today, as we did, for a corner design for "High Hatters," page 6, or for any other design that suits your fancy.

CIRCLES AND SQUARES, *design plate, page 72; photo, page 6.*

This design originated as a pattern for weaving on netted fabric. Its contemporary interpretation is a needlepoint border for the "High Hatters" shown on page 6.

BIRD TALK *(2-1/2″ x 3-1/2″), design plate, page 71; photo, page 67.*
ELEPHANT PARADE *(2-1/2″ x 3-1/2″), design plate, page 69; photo, page 67.*
PETER COTTONTAIL *(2-1/2″ x 2-1/2″), design plate, page 68; photo, page 67.*

A SQUIRREL'S CHRISTMAS *(3″ x 4″), design plate, page 69; photo, page 67.*

These four designs appear as needlepoint Christmas tree ornaments, but would be right at home as tiny pictures for a child's room. To make them, work design in needlepoint, back with felt (page 94), and add a yarn loop for hanging.

FULL SAIL, *design plate, page 70.*
LITTLE LOCOMOTIVE, *design plate, page 70.*

These two designs from the 1920's were originally intended for borders of cross-stitch on napkins and tea towels. Today, they're perfect for cross-stitch embroidery on children's clothing. Or, use them with several of the other whimsical designs for a gingham quilt like the Alphabet Quilt shown on page 46.

HAPPY HEART, *design plate, page 69; photo, page 67.*

The heart, the traditional symbol of love and devotion, appears here for the sewing basket as a needlepoint pincushion. On #10 canvas, work four "Happy Hearts" as shown in the photograph, add cording, back with a scrap of red corduroy, and stuff tightly.

DIAMONDS, *design plate, page 72.*

This design originally appeared in 1926 as a border pattern in a knitted sweater. Try it as a border or allover pattern in needlepoint.

MISTER RABBIT, *design plate, page 68.*

"Mister Rabbit" nibbles on a carrot in true rabbit fashion. He originally appeared as a design for cross-stitch in a 1924 issue of Butterick's *Needle-Arts* magazine.

WISE-EYED OWLS, *design plate, page 71.*

A friend who fancies owls would love these little birds on a needlepoint or cross-stitch picture or greeting card.

BUTTERFLY BAND, *design plate, page 71.*

A pretty butterfly from a 1920's pattern for crochet edging to work in cross-stitch or needlepoint, alone or in a border.

CHRISTMAS CANDLE, *design plate, page 70.*

Use this original cross-stitch design for a Christmas tree ornament like those shown on page 67.

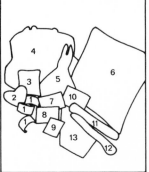

Proud Parent

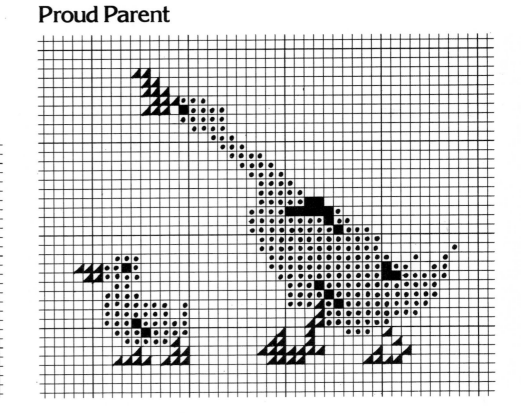

Peter Cottontail

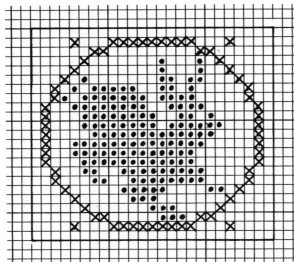

What's For Lunch?

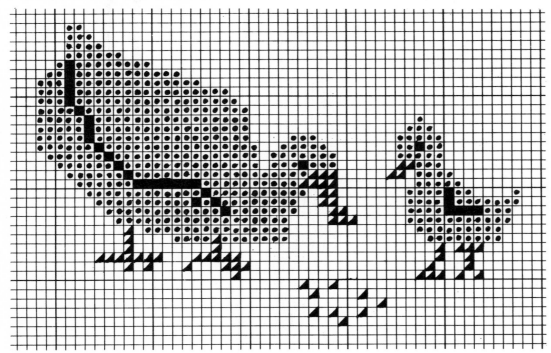

Mister Rabbit

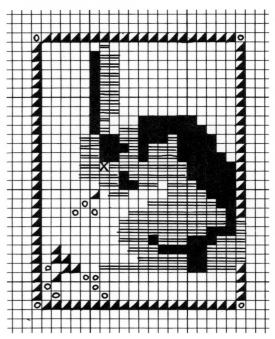

For graph color key, see page 82.

All designs which appear on graphs were done in the scale of 10 stitches per inch. Designs may be worked on any size canvas but size of completed work will change accordingly.

Floral Corner

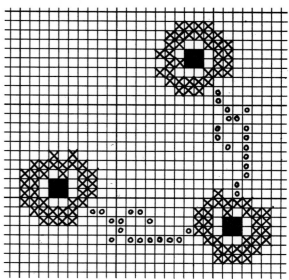

Puzzle

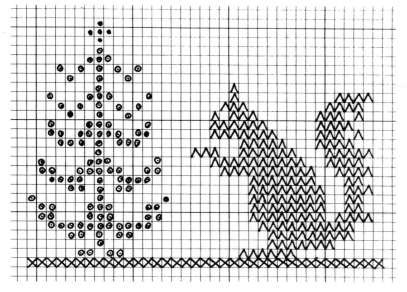

A Squirrel's Christmas

Elephant Parade

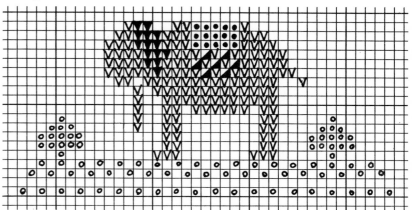

Happy Heart

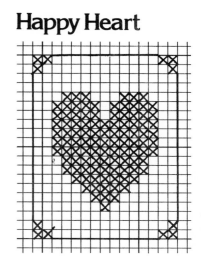

Floral Border

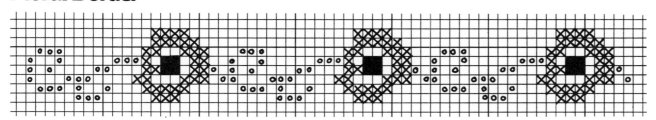

For graph color key, see page 82.

All designs which appear on graphs were done in the scale of 10 stitches per inch. Designs may be worked on any size canvas but size of completed work will change accordingly.

Fruit and Flowers

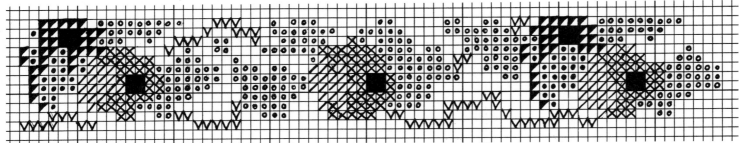

Full Sail

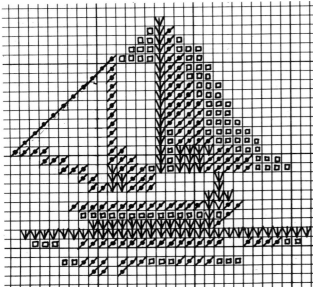

All designs which appear on graphs were done in the scale of 10 stitches per inch. Designs may be worked on any size canvas but size of completed work will change accordingly.

Christmas Bells

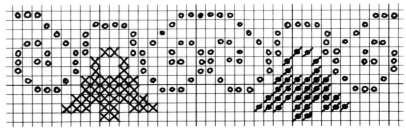

Little Locomotive

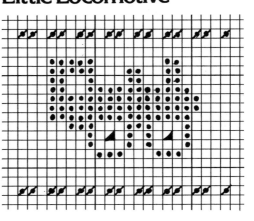

All Aboard

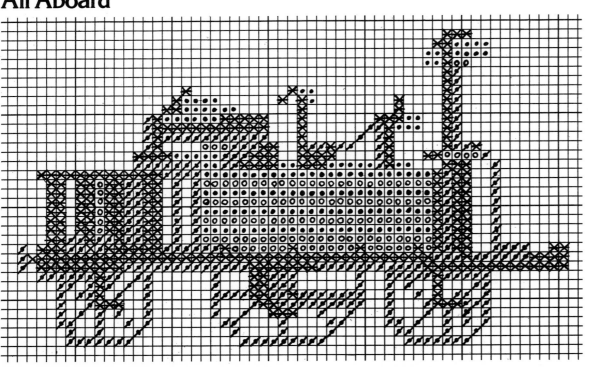

For graph color key, see page 82.

Christmas Candle

Wise-Eyed Owls

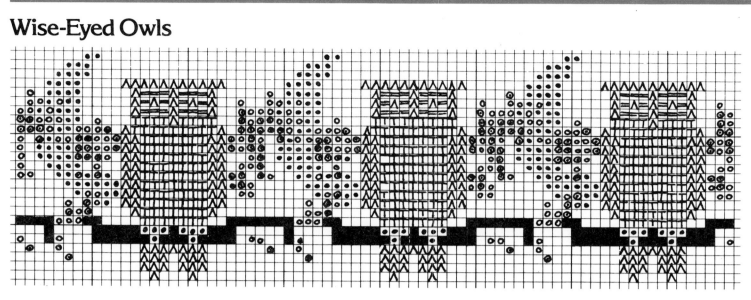

Butterfly Band

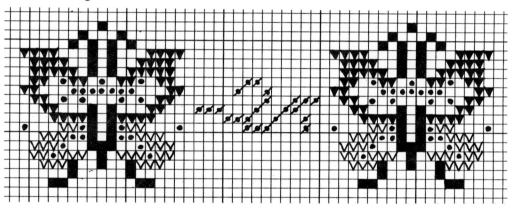

Bird Talk

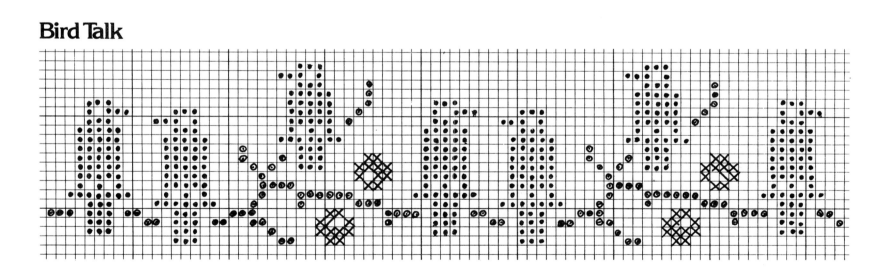

All designs which appear on graphs were done in the scale of 10 stitches per inch. Designs may be worked on any size canvas but size of completed work will change accordingly.

For graph color key, see page 82.

Rick Rack

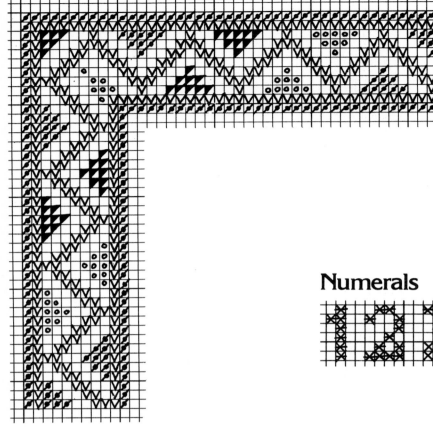

Martha Washington Rose

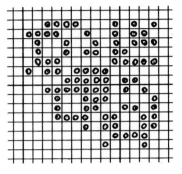

Numerals

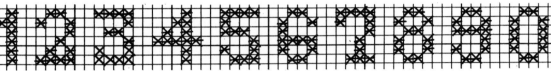

Circles and Squares

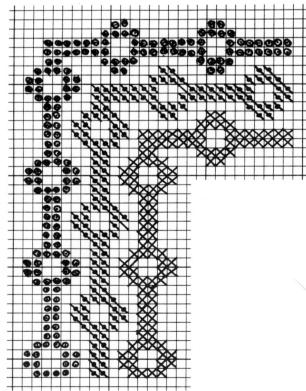

Diamonds

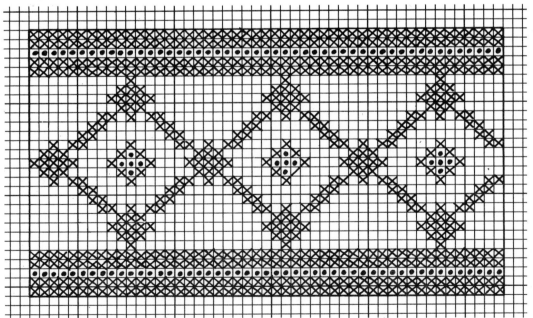

All designs which appear on graphs were done in the scale of 10 stitches per inch. Designs may be worked on any size canvas but size of completed work will change accordingly.

For graph color key, see page 82.

3
Needlework Materials and Techniques

The resurgence in the popularity of needlework today is related to the climate of our society. Manufactured goods turned out by the thousands have a certain coldness and lack personality. Needlework is a very personal statement so it adds individuality and warmth wherever it is used.

The end use of a needlework project is an important consideration and should influence the project from its beginning. Style, size, and color are all dependent on how the project will be used. Since designs may be executed in several different techniques and in many materials, it is important to decide how the needlework will be used and then, plan the project around that purpose. What colors and patterns will be used with the needlework? Will it be the focus of attention or just an accent? Will it require frequent care due to soil and wear? How durable must it be? Answers to these and any other pertinent questions will guide you to the materials, design, techniques, and finishing that will be perfect for your purpose.

Needlework can be used almost anywhere. It can add a decorative accent to your wardrobe. Use it on jeans, shirts, vests, pants, blouses, dresses, ties, sweaters, shawls ... everywhere. The tremendous range of de-

signs, styles, materials, and techniques means you can add your personal touch to almost any garment. Needlework is great for accessories, too. It can highlight hats, headbands, scarves, patches, socks, tennis shoes, belts, purses and totes, and luggage. In the home, needlework can be used for table appointments, furnishings, decorative accessories such as pillows, mirror and picture frames, room dividers, wall hangings, quilts and other bed coverings, rugs and curtains. There are many suggestions for each design in *Needlework Nostalgia*.

For many of the designs and projects in this book, color suggestions are included. However, reaction to color and color combinations is a highly personal response based on preference, perception, and past experience. Experiment with color because light, yarn texture and weight, the interaction of one color with another, and even the stitches used can change the color effect. Coordinate your needlework with your room, your favorite garment or accessory, or your mood! Today, rules about color and color usage have changed radically or been discarded entirely. So, make your color decisions from a unique personal interpretation of color and its meanings for you.

The following sections contain easy-to-follow guides

Needlework Nostalgia

for the techniques of embroidery, needlepoint, appliqué, patchwork, and quilting. Also included are instructions for enlarging and reducing designs and for transferring designs to fabric or canvas. Finally, there are instructions for finishing and mounting needlework as pillows or wall hangings and for adding such finishing touches as fringe, ruffles, and cording which can complete a project with a high note of decorative excitement.

Enlarging or Reducing Designs

Use a simple grid system of perfect squares. A design can be translated to any size, larger or smaller, by using a grid. The determining factor is the relationship between the grid size of the original design and the grid size to which it is transferred. Determine how much to enlarge or reduce the design by considering the size of the completed project and the size relationship between completed size and the design size given on the design plate.

Decide on the design to be enlarged or reduced. Both simple, single element motifs and more complex designs can be reduced or enlarged by the grid method.

Place a grid over the design. The grid should consist of carefully measured exact squares.

Note: A short cut is to overlay original design with transparent graph paper or fine wire screen. The design may also be drawn onto graph paper eliminating the need to painstakingly construct grids.

Prepare a grid with the same number of squares as the grid superimposed over the design. Number the squares along the side and letter the top on both grids for easy reference while drawing. Be precise in constructing the grid because the "look" of the enlarged or reduced design depends on exactly duplicating the design from one grid square to another of identical proportions.

To enlarge design:
The prepared grid should have larger squares than the original design. If the design to be enlarged is superimposed with a grid of 1/8″ squares, translate it onto a grid of 1/4″, 1/2″, or 1″ squares.

To reduce design:
The prepared grid should have smaller squares than the original design. If the design to be reduced is superimposed with a grid of 1″ squares, translate it onto a grid of 1/2″, 1/4″, or 1/8″ squares.

Translate outline to grid one square at a time.
Follow design carefully checking square by square as you go.

Designs may also be enlarged or reduced by "photostating." Photostating is a photographic process that produces a negative image (white lines on a black background) or a positive image (black lines on a white background) in matte or glossy finish. Ask for a positive image because it is easier to work with and matte finish because it is usually less expensive. Techniques for indicating the desired increase or decrease in size vary from one company to another. Decide the size you want. Dimensions and instructions will be written on the original. You will receive both your original design and the finished "stat." If you would like to reverse the direction of a design, tell the photostat house that you want the design to be a reverse image of the original. Greatly reducing or enlarging the design may produce a photostat in which the lines are not crisp and smooth. Because transferring a design accurately requires a crisp, smooth line, place tracing paper over the photostat and fill in the line by tracing over it.

Find a source for photostating by checking the yellow pages of your phone directory under "photocopying."

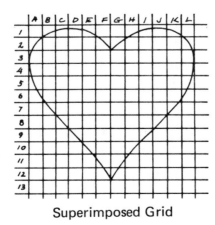

Superimposed Grid

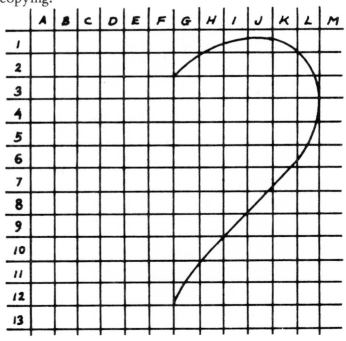

Translating Design to New Grid

Transferring Designs to Fabric

There are many methods of transferring a design to fabric. A quick easy one is tracing.

You will need:
☆ Dressmaker's Carbon
   Note: Do not use ordinary carbon paper. Dressmaker's carbon is designed for use on fabric and the range of colors allows transfer to both light and dark fabrics.
☆ Pencil, Stylus, or Tracing Wheel
☆ Tracing paper

To transfer design:
☆ Trace design from book or photostat onto tracing paper.
☆ Draw centerline horizontally and vertically on design.
☆ Baste a horizontal and vertical centerline on fabric.
☆ Tape fabric to hard, flat surface with right side up.
☆ Place design on fabric matching centerlines.
☆ Secure design in place with tape on two adjacent sides.
☆ Slip dressmaker's carbon between fabric and design. *Be sure to place waxed side of carbon paper next to fabric.*
☆ Go over all design lines with pencil, stylus, or tracing wheel. Check to see if enough pressure is being applied to transfer the design to the fabric. Start at the top and work down to prevent smudging the lines with the pressure and movement of your hand. Use the pencil or stylus for complex designs and the tracing wheel for simple designs.
☆ When all design lines are transferred, remove carbon and tape.

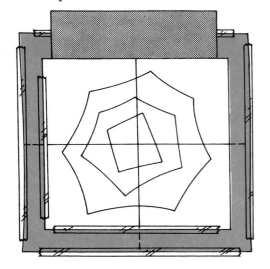

Positioning Design and Carbon for Tracing

For sheer or transparent fabrics and needlepoint canvas, it is easiest to trace directly from the design illustration. Use a pencil or chalk to trace onto fabric. Use a *waterproof* felt tip pen to trace onto needlepoint canvas because the moisture necessary for blocking a canvas will make some inks run and ruin the canvas.

To transfer the design:
☆ Place fabric or canvas over the design. Be careful to allow an extra 2″ on all sides for a margin.
☆ Paper clip the page and the fabric (or canvas) together so that they will not slip as you trace.
☆ Trace each design line with pen, pencil, or chalk.
☆ Remove fabric.

Another method employs a running stitch. Use this method when other marking methods would permanently mar the fabric. Trace the design onto lightweight paper such as tissue paper.

To transfer design:
☆ Draw centerline vertically and horizontally on tissue paper.
☆ Baste centerline vertically and horizontally on fabric.
☆ Match lines and pin or baste together.
☆ Outline the design with running stitches made through tissue paper *and* fabric. More than one color thread may be used to indicate yarn colors or to distinguish parts of the design.
☆ When marking is completed, gently tear the tissue away.

In needlework such as appliqué, quilting, and patchwork where motifs are repeated, templates are useful for drawing the designs directly on the fabric. Templates can be made of brown paper, oak tag, or sandpaper. The brown paper can be pinned to fabric. Oak tag can be pinned or held in place. The grit of the sandpaper helps to hold it on the fabric. With either oak tag or sandpaper, the design template will be durable enough to use several times. When the edges become frayed, bent, or crumpled, discard the templates because accurate marking will be impossible. (Metal, plastic, and paper templates are made commmercially in the most common designs and are available in needlework shops and department stores.) The first step in making a template is to draw or trace each shape on graph paper. Use a T-square, protractor, plastic triangle, and ruler to ensure accuracy. Cut out graph paper shapes and glue them on template material. Accuracy in measuring, transferring, and marking are important in appliqué and quilting but are *essential* to patchwork. For most hand appliqué, machine appliqué, and patchwork, make templates by either of the following methods.

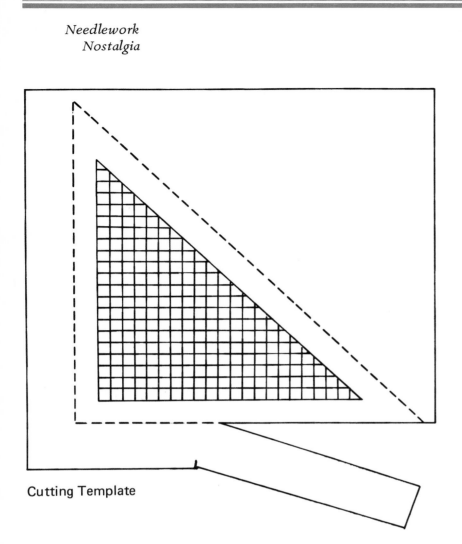

Cutting Template

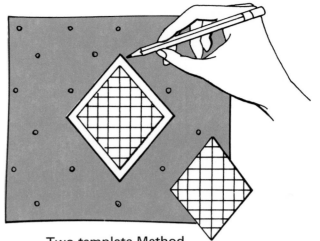

Two-template Method

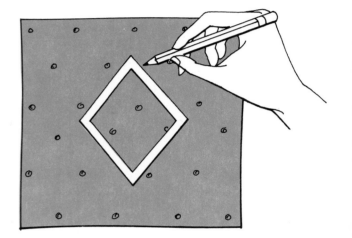

Window Template Method

Method One:

Make two templates. One template should be a duplicate of the design and the other template the design plus seam allowances. (Seam allowances for patchwork and appliqué are usually 1/4″ or 3/8″ wide.) To mark fabric, trace around the largest template first. To mark seam allowances, center the other template within the marked area and trace around it.

Method Two:

Make a window template. Transfer design plus seam allowances to template material and cut out. Then, remove the actual design from the center with scissors or a utility knife. Be sure the template is accurate and allow for the space of marking with a pencil or waterproof felt tip. Mark the cutting line on the fabric by tracing around the outside and the seamline by tracing around the inside of the template. Use Method One for making templates for very large designs as a window template may be too flimsy for accurate marking.

For some machine appliqué, appliqué with fusibles, and quilting, no seam allowance or turn-under allowance is required. Cut out template, place on fabric, and simply trace around the outside. Use a pencil. A waterproof marking pen can be used if marking is on the wrong side of the fabric and will not show.

Needle Essentials

Choosing the right needle for the type of needlework you are planning is extremely important. For example, a heavy darning needle with its large eye is too thick for embroidery on fine linen or percale because it would leave large holes in your work and cause puckering. Generally, the finer or sheerer the fabric, the sharper and more slender the needle should be. Needles come in sizes ranging from 1 to 24. The smaller the number of the needle, the longer and coarser it is.

For embroidery, use embroidery/crewel needles. They are slender with a sharp point and a long eye and are available in a wide range of sizes suitable for use with many types of fabric, yarn, or thread.

Tapestry needles, which are short and heavy with large eyes and blunt points, are ideal for needlepoint.

Sharps are recommended for hand sewing for appliqué, patchwork, and quilting. They are medium-length needles with small rounded eyes for general sewing.

To thread a needle . . .

Method One:

Push yarn end through eye of needle. Many threads and yarns are threaded easily this way.

Method Two:

Loop yarn around needle and hold near the fold. Then slip yarn off needle and push fold through eye of the needle. Thick, bulky yarns are threaded this way.

Method Three:

For thick yarn that is difficult to push through the needle when doubled and creased, use a folded paper. Cut a rectangle of lightweight paper which is approximately twice the diameter of the yarn and about a half inch long. Fold paper lengthwise. Place yarn inside folded paper, press closed, and slide yarn and paper through needle eye. Each paper can be used again but to save time, cut several at the beginning of each work session.

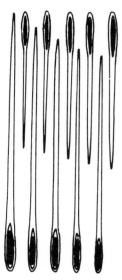

Tapestry Needles

Embroidery Needles

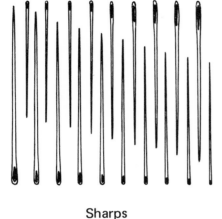

Sharps

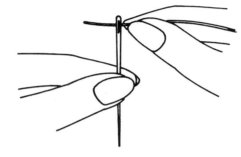

Method One

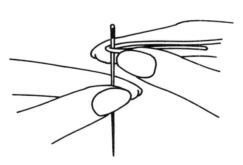

Method Two

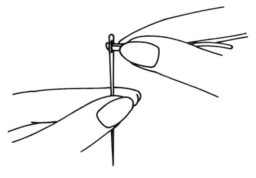

Method Three

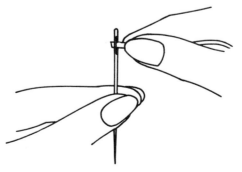

*Needlework
Nostalgia*

Embroidery

Embroidery is the surface decoration of fabric using a needle threaded with yarn, thread, or cord. There are several hundred embroidery stitches but many are variations of a few basic stitches. These stitches may be used for many different kinds of embroidery. For example, crewel embroidery means embroidery done with a particular wool yarn called crewel yarn. Cross-stitch embroidery refers to a counted thread embroidery done with the cross-stitch exclusively. There are many other kinds of embroidery.

Materials:

☆ Fabric
Fabric for embroidery should be smooth and loosely woven so that yarn pulls through easily. Suggested fabrics include linen, cotton (broadcloth, percale, denim), and burlap. Many fabrics are suitable for embroidery and the fabric must be coordinated with the weight and texture of the yarn to be used.

☆ Yarn, Thread, Cord
Many kinds of yarns are used for embroidery. Some common ones are embroidery floss, matte cotton, pearl cotton, crewel yarn, tapestry yarn. Even cord such as macramé cord that is too thick to be pulled through fabric can be used for couching (see stitches below). Gold and silver threads may also be used for couching.

☆ Needles
Embroidery/crewel needles (see page 76) are slender with a sharp point and a long eye. They are available in a wide range of sizes and are suitable for use with many types of fabric, yarn, and thread.
  Tapestry needles (see page 76) have a blunt point and large eye. Use them with very loosely woven fabric and thick yarns.

☆ Hoops
Hoops are essential in embroidery because they hold the fabric taut while stitching and help the stitcher control tension. Metal, plastic, and wood hoops are available in a wide range of sizes but wood hoops are usually more reliable and easier to use. Always buy hoops with an adjustable screw to allow accommodation of a variety of fabrics.

The Stitches*

Running Stitch

Move needle in and out of fabric one stitch at a time.

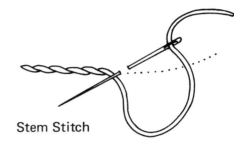

Stem Stitch

Put needle in fabric at stitch length position and bring it out in middle of stitch. (Yarn can be held above or below stitch, but this should be consistent.)

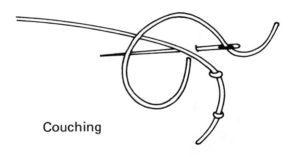

Couching

Couching attaches yarn to fabric with another yarn. Lay yarn to be couched on fabric. Attach by stitching across the couched yarn at intervals.

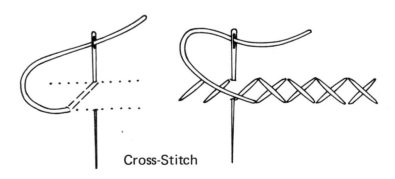

Cross-Stitch

Make diagonal stitch and cross it with another diagonal stitch.
  For cross-stitch rows, make row of diagonal stitches. Cross each stitch in row with another diagonal stitch.

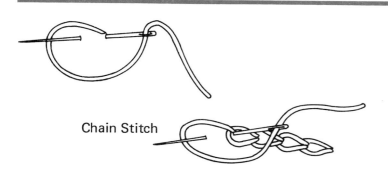

Chain Stitch

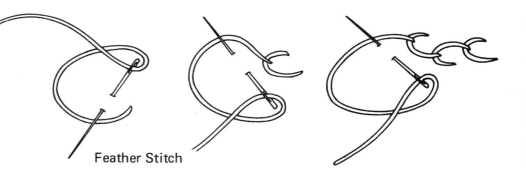

Feather Stitch

Put needle in next to up-coming yarn and bring it out at stitch length position. Loop yarn under needle. Pull needle through.

Next, put needle in link next to up-coming yarn. Bring needle up at stitch length position. Loop yarn under needle. Pull needle through.

Make a stitch diagonal to up-coming yarn. Loop yarn under the needle. Pull needle through.

Place next stitch diagonally to first. Loop yarn under needle. Pull needle through.

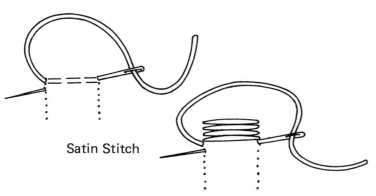

Satin Stitch

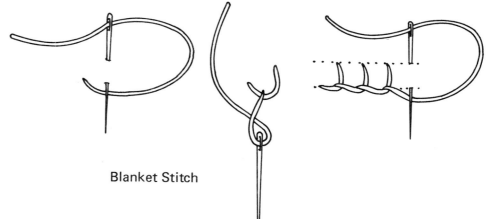

Blanket Stitch

Insert needle for stitch length. Carry yarn behind work and bring up in position for next stitch.

Stitches should be close together and make a smooth surface.

Make vertical stitch so needle passes over loop of yarn.

Pull needle through.

*These are the basic embroidery stitches you might use to execute the designs in *Needlework Nostalgia*. There are many more.

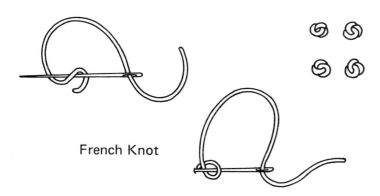

French Knot

Wind yarn around needle one to three times.

Insert needle next to up-coming yarn. Hold yarn firmly as needle is drawn down through coiled yarn.

Use the French knot individually or in groups.

Technique:
1. Press fabric. Transfer design to fabric.
2. Assemble hoops and fabric. Move hoops from one area to another as work progresses. To protect the completed stitching, tissue paper may be placed between the hoops and stitches. Always remove hoops at the end of a work session to prevent hard creases from forming in the fabric.
3. Begin embroidery by tying a knot in the end of the yarn and passing the yarn from the right side to the underside of the fabric about 1/2 inch from the starting point on a design line. Take a few embroidery stitches along the design line catching the yarn with each stitch. When you reach the knot, clip it off. The yarn will be secured on the underside by the stitches. As you finish each yarn, weave the yarn end into a few stitches on the back of the work. (Knots to begin and end a yarn are not usually recommended because they

Needlework Nostalgia

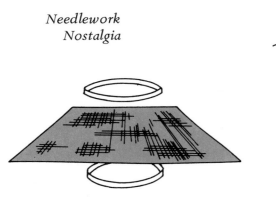

Press hoops together.

Place fabric between hoops with the larger hoop above and smaller hoop below fabric.

Fabric should be taut and smooth.

may untie allowing pulled stitches which ultimately destroy the piece. They may also create lumps in your work.)

4. If the embroidery is soiled when completed, wash it by hand in lukewarm water and mild soap. Squeeze fabric but do not rub or twist. Be sure to rinse well. Roll in a towel to dry. Press on wrong side while still slightly damp. Use a thick pad, such as a terry towel, between the stitches and the ironing board to prevent flattening the stitches.

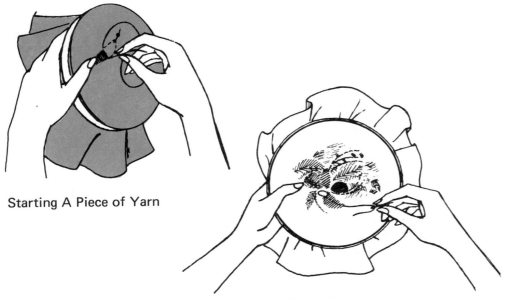

Starting A Piece of Yarn

Ending A Piece of Yarn

Even after pressing, embroidery may still be puckered. Puckering occurs when a yarn pushes threads in the fabric aside and when tension is tight on the stitches. Blocking may be necessary.

To block embroidery:

1. Cover a soft wood board with brown paper. The paper protects the embroidery from stains in the wood.
2. Mark the exact dimensions of the embroidery on the paper with a pencil and check with a T-square to square corners.
3. Block embroidery by stretching it to match the square markings and thumbtacking it to the board. Always use rust-proof tacks to avoid rust marks. Tack one edge at a time working from the center to each corner.
4. Sponge the embroidery with warm water and allow to dry at least 24 hours.
5. Remove from board.

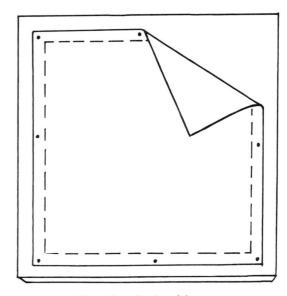

Blocking Embroidery

Tips for Cross-Stitch:

Since cross-stitch embroidery is counted-thread embroidery, use an even-weave fabric. Gingham is a traditional choice because the checks provide a guide for the stitches, but any even-weave fabric with threads that can be counted is suitable. With gingham, interesting shaded effects are obtained by using the blocks in a planned way (for example, locating the majority of the stitches in white blocks). The most popular and traditional size gingham to use is 1/8″ checks but motifs can be greatly changed in size and effect by using larger checks.

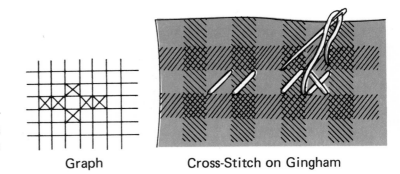

Graph   Cross-Stitch on Gingham

Cross-stitch can be worked from a graph. Each square of the graph represents a counted square of fabric (or a check in the case of gingham). Symbols in graph squares represent stitches. Open graph squares indicate areas where no stitches are to be taken.

Needlepoint

Needlepoint is a counted-thread embroidery on even-weave fabric or stiff canvas. Needlepoint can be pictorial or geometric. Geometric patterns, usually done with vertical and horizontal stitches, are called bargello. Petit point, gros point, and quick point are names given to types of needlepoint distinguished by the size mesh and number of stitches they require. Petit point is worked on fine canvas, 16 or more mesh per inch; gros point is worked on 8 to 15 mesh per inch canvas; quick point is worked on canvas with 3 to 5 mesh per inch.

Materials:
☆ Canvas
Needlepoint canvas is a cotton fabric woven in open, regular squares and stiffened for body and easy stitching. The size of canvas describes the number of mesh (threads) per inch. For example, #10 canvas has 10 mesh to the inch while #16 canvas has 16 mesh to the inch. Canvas ranges in size from very coarse, #3 to very fine, #40 and is sold by the yard.

There are two basic types of canvas:
Duo (double-threaded canvas). Duo canvas has two threads for each mesh so that it can be split for finer detail in selected areas of the design or be used for petit point. This canvas is also commonly called Penelope canvas.

Mono (single-threaded canvas). Mono canvas has one thread for each mesh and is suitable for many designs. Bargello should *always* be worked on mono canvas because of its strict geometry.

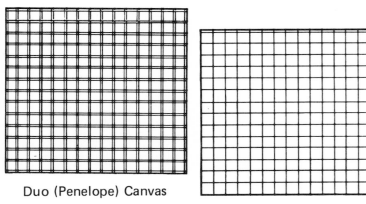

Duo (Penelope) Canvas

Mono Canvas

☆ Yarn
Many yarns in a wide array of colors are available for needlepoint. Although it is difficult to estimate the amount of yarn needed for a design it is better to buy too much rather than too little because variations in dye lots make it difficult to match colors. Left-over yarn is ideal for creating small needlepoint projects like napkin rings, coasters, and eyeglass cases. Most salesclerks can help you estimate the amount of yarn needed so take the design with you to purchase yarn. Needlepoint yarn calculators are also available. Or, you can estimate the amount needed yourself. Simply calculate the number of square inches to be covered by each color. Make generous estimates for oddly shaped areas. Multiply the number of square inches for each color by the amount of yarn needed to cover one square inch of canvas. Since this amount will vary with the stitch used and the canvas size (mesh per inch), it will be necessary to work a square inch of canvas to determine how much yarn it takes.

Three of the yarn types most commonly used for needlepoint include:
Persian Wool—A three-stranded yarn, Persian wool can be divided easily for use on several canvas sizes.

Tapestry Wool—A four-ply yarn that is tightly twisted, tapestry wool is not easily separated and is not used on canvas smaller than 14 mesh per inch.

Crewel Yarn—A fine, two-ply yarn, crewel can be used with several threads together to cover many different sizes of canvas.

Other interesting yarn possibilities are rug wool, stranded cotton, gold and silver thread, chenille, embroidery floss, and pearl cotton.

☆ Needles
For needlepoint use tapestry needles. (See page 76.)

☆ The Stitches
The needlepoint stitches illustrated here are some of the basic and most often used. There are many others. The stitch illustrations are numbered for easy translation.

Odd numbers indicate that the needle is coming to the front of the work at the beginning of a stitch.

Even numbers indicate that the needle is going to the back of the canvas at the completion of a stitch.

Numbers which are turned upside down indicate that the canvas and the stitch illustration should be turned to complete the stitch.

Needlework Nostalgia

The first three stitches illustrated, Continental, Basket Weave, and Half Cross, are the ones most often used and all three create the same appearance on the surface of the work. The Half Cross-Stitch requires the least amount of yarn and results in the thinnest completed fabric. It is best used for needlepoint pictures and articles which will receive little wear. It should be worked only on Duo (Penelope) canvas. The Continental Stitch and the Basket Weave Stitch require more yarn because they create a padded effect on the back of the work which increases the durability and wearing qualities of the finished work. Continental Stitch is best used for outlining, for working fine details, and for filling in small areas. If it is used for the entire work, the canvas will become badly misshapen and require extensive blocking. The Basket Weave Stitch is recommended for filling in backgrounds as well as any other areas of the design.

The remainder of the stitches illustrated here are known as fancy needlepoint stitches and are recommended to add texture and variety to your work.

Technique:
1. Cut canvas to size allowing a two-inch border all around for blocking, mounting, and stitch shrinkage (canvas is drawn up when stitches are taken). For a ten-inch square design, canvas should be cut fourteen inches square. Bind the edges with masking tape to prevent raveling and to make the canvas easier to hold.
2. Transfer design to canvas by tracing design onto the canvas with waterproof markers (refer to page 75). If you wish, the canvas may be painted to indicate colors. Use waterproof pens or acrylic paint. To avoid clogging the canvas, make certain the paint is not too thick. Several designs in this book appear in graph form which does not require direct tracing onto the canvas. Reading a graph is quite simple if you remember one simple convention. *Each square of the graph represents an intersection of threads in the canvas.* Always count intersections of the canvas threads (mesh)

Graph Color Key

WHITE ⊟
LIGHT GREY ⊞
DARK GREY ◨
BLACK ■
FLESH ⊡
BEIGE ⊓
BROWN ◩
LIGHT YELLOW ⊞
MEDIUM YELLOW ⊡
DARK YELLOW ⊞
ORANGE ◪
PINK ◨
MEDIUM RED ⊠
DARK RED ⊗
MAUVE ▼
PURPLE ▽
LIGHT GREEN ⊞
MEDIUM GREEN ⊙
DARK GREEN ◉
LIGHT BLUE ▫
MEDIUM BLUE ◨
DARK BLUE ▼

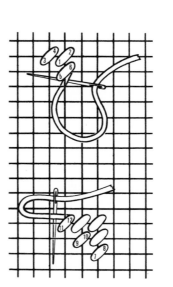
Half Cross-Stitch

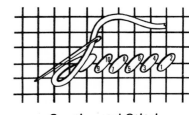
Continental Stitch

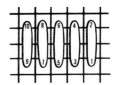
Upright Gobelin Stitch

Cross-Stitch

Basket Weave Stitch

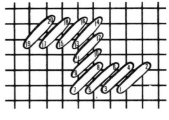
Byzantine Stitch

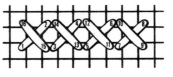
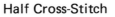

not holes in the canvas. When working from a graph, locate the center of the graph and the center of the canvas and begin there.

The colors used on the graphs which appear on several design plates are suggestions only. Samples which appear in color photography were not necessarily worked in the same colors as those which appear on the graphs since individual color preference dictates color choice.

3. Before you begin to stitch, try the yarn, stitches, and needle to be certain that all function well together to cover the canvas smoothly and easily. To begin stitching, tie a knot in the end of a piece of yarn and pass the yarn from the right side to the underside of the canvas about one-half inch from the beginning point. Take a few stitches along the row catching the yarn with each stitch. When you reach the knot, clip it off. The yarn will be secured on the underside by the stitches. As you finish each yarn, pass the yarn end under

a few stitches on the back of the work. Begin and end subsequent yarns by passing the yarn end under a few stitches on the back of the work.

Begin working in the center of the canvas and work the design areas first and the background last. If the design includes curves and diagonals, remember that needlepoint canvas is basically geometric and that curves and diagonals are made up of small geometric steps that give the appearance of a curve.

4. After you complete the needlepoint, it may be soiled and misshapen. Have it dry cleaned by a specialist or use one of the commercial products made especially for this use. Blocking is necessary to restore the desired shape to the canvas and to set the stitches for a finished appearance.

To block a canvas:
Draw the exact dimensions of the needlepoint on brown paper. Be sure that the drawing is

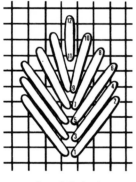

Leaf Stitch

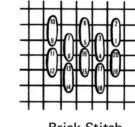

Slanted Gobelin Stitch

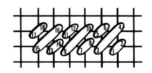

Brick Stitch

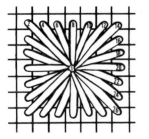

Eyelet Stitch

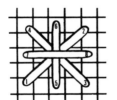

Double Cross-Stitch

Mosiac Stitch

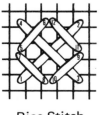

Rice Stitch

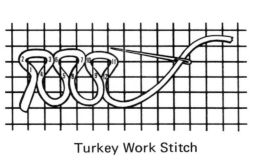

Turkey Work Stitch

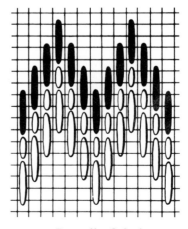

Bargello Stitch

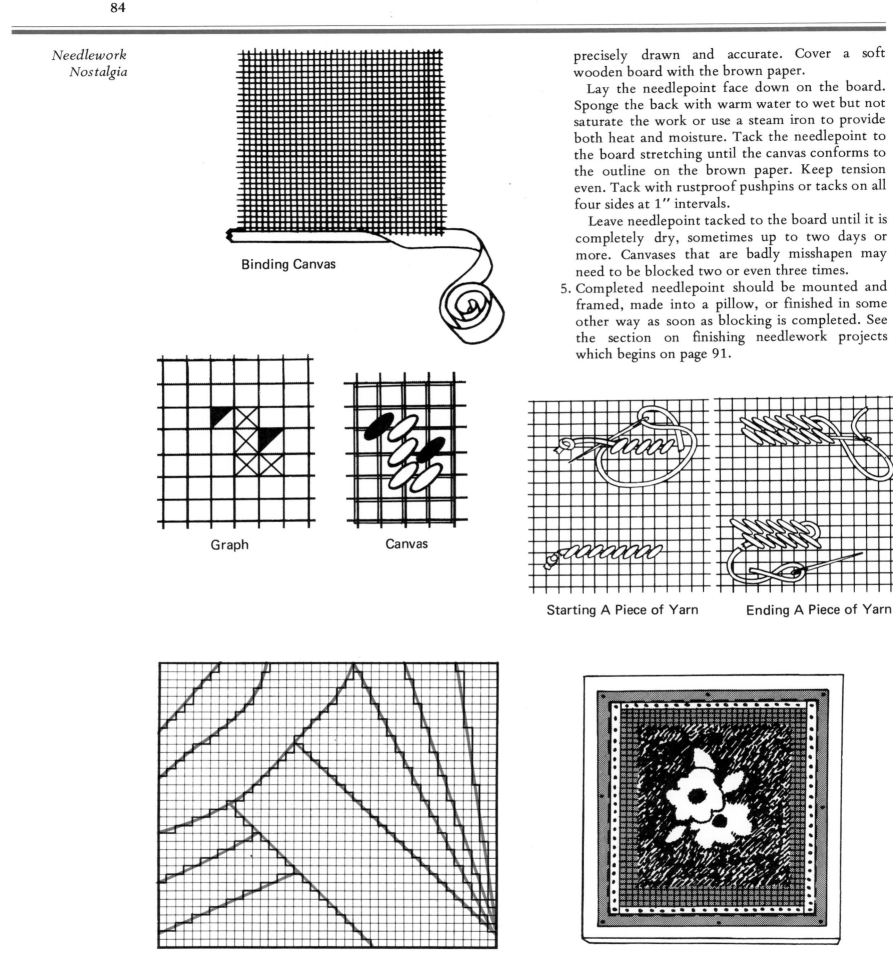

Binding Canvas

Graph   Canvas

Starting A Piece of Yarn   Ending A Piece of Yarn

Interaction of Curves and Diagonals on Graph

Blocking Needlepoint

precisely drawn and accurate. Cover a soft wooden board with the brown paper.

Lay the needlepoint face down on the board. Sponge the back with warm water to wet but not saturate the work or use a steam iron to provide both heat and moisture. Tack the needlepoint to the board stretching until the canvas conforms to the outline on the brown paper. Keep tension even. Tack with rustproof pushpins or tacks on all four sides at 1″ intervals.

Leave needlepoint tacked to the board until it is completely dry, sometimes up to two days or more. Canvases that are badly misshapen may need to be blocked two or even three times.

5. Completed needlepoint should be mounted and framed, made into a pillow, or finished in some other way as soon as blocking is completed. See the section on finishing needlework projects which begins on page 91.

Appliqué

Appliqué is attaching one or more fabric pieces to a background fabric to create a design. Fabrics may be attached using various hand stitches or machine stitches or with a fusible bonding agent. Appliqué and embroidery are often used together because they complement each other. Appliqué provides large, bold shapes and embroidery adds linear interest and texture. Several samples in *Needlework Nostalgia* combine these techniques.

Materials:
☆ Fabric
Fabric for appliqué should be firm and smooth and resistant to fraying. Suggested fabrics include percale, broadcloth, felt, and some linens and wools. Many fabrics are suitable for one appliqué technique and not for another, so fabric and technique should be coordinated.

☆ Yarn
The thread or yarn used depends on the appliqué technique chosen. For hand appliqué and machine appliqué, use either cotton-covered polyester or mercerized cotton sewing thread. When embroidery stitches are combined with appliqué, any thread or yarn suitable for embroidery can be used. Using a fusible *bonding* agent (see below) eliminates thread except for embroidery stitches that may be added to enhance the appliqué.

☆ Needles
Needles for appliqué are also dependent on the technique. Use hand sewing needles called sharps for hand appliqué. Use embroidery/crewel needles for embroidery. (See page 76.) And, of course, machine needles for machine embroidery, usually size 14.

☆ Fusibles
A fusible bonding agent is a lightweight, thermoplastic web that joins two fabrics by fusing when heat, moisture, and pressure are applied with an iron. These bonding agents are marketed in several widths and lengths and are usually available where fabrics are sold. (Current brand names of this material include Pellon's Fusible Web, Stacy's Stitch Witchery, and Poly Bond by Coats and Clark.)

Technique:
Appliqué by hand with a turned edge.
1. Press fabric.
2. Transfer design to background fabric for placement of each appliqué. Transfer individual appliqué designs to selected fabrics. Add 1/4" turn-under allowance to each appliqué. For design motifs that appear several times in a design or motifs that will be reused for multiple projects, see directions for making templates on page 76.
3. Stitch around each appliqué on the seamline by hand or machine. Use this stitching as a guide for placing appliqué on the background and for turning under the edge.
4. Turn edges and press lightly.
5. Pin appliqué in place.
6. Stitch each part of the appliqué in place with a slip stitch, running stitch or other embroidery stitch like the blanket stitch, for example.

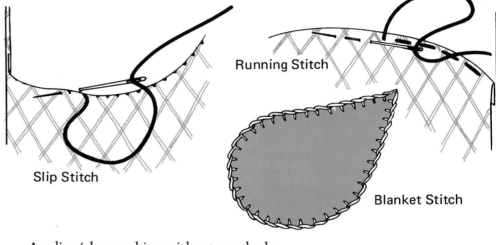

Slip Stitch Running Stitch Blanket Stitch

Appliqué by machine with a turned edge.
1. Transfer design to appliqué fabric. A turned edge requires a 1/4" turn-under allowance on all sides of the shape.
2. Turn under the edge and press.
3. Position appliqué on background fabric.
4. Straight stitch close to edge or use a narrow zig-zag stitch.

Straight Stitch Zig-Zag Stitch

Turning points and curves precisely on appliqué pieces is a frequent problem. To make a sharp point on a turned edge, use the three-fold method. First, fold the point down on the turn-under allowance line. Then, fold

Needlework Nostalgia

one side toward the center. Fold in the other side until the edges meet at the center of the point. Crease.

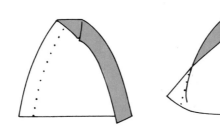

Three-fold Method

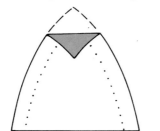

Clipping Curves

To turn under a curved edge, clip. The more curved an area is, the more clips are necessary. Clip as you work to prevent fraying.

Appliqué by machine without a turned edge.
1. Transfer design to appliqué fabric. Cut out appliqué leaving a margin of fabric all around it.
2. Position the fabric with the design in place on background fabric and baste with one of the following techniques.

    Machine baste with straight stitch on design line.

    Machine baste with zig-zag on design line.

    Heat baste with fusible bonding agent by snipping a small piece of the web and placing it between the appliqué and the background fabric. Follow product directions for fusing. Allow to cool. Appliqué will be held in place but the appliqué edges will be free making machine or hand stitching easier.
3. Then use either Method One or Method Two:*

Method One:
Satin stitch over basting line.
Trim fabric away close to the stitching.
Note: Illustration shows straight stitch basting. Zig-zag stitch or heat basting could also be used.

    *Skilled seamstresses may find the basting and trimming stages illustrated unnecessary. Simply, cut out the appliqué on the design line, position appliqué on background fabric, and satin stitch to attach it.

Method Two:
Trim close to basted line.
Satin stitch over basting to enclose raw edge.
Note: Illustration shows zig-zag basting. Straight stitch or heat basting could also be used.

Tips for satin stitching:
Go slowly!
For smooth curves, stop machine with needle in outside edge of satin stitch. Lift foot and pivot *fabric slightly.* Lower foot. Turn wheel by hand for a few stitches. Repeat as often as necessary to follow curves or corners. Machine stitches should be at right angles to the fabric edge.

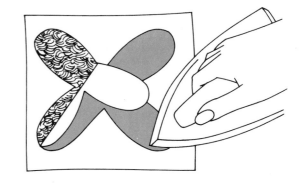

Fusing Appliqué

Appliqué with fusibles.
1. Transfer design to appliqué fabric and to fusible web. Cut out carefully.
2. Place fusible bonding agent between the appliqué and background fabric and follow product directions for fusing. (A paper towel placed between the iron and the appliqué will help prevent the bonding agent from sticking to the iron soleplate.) Allow to cool on the ironing board to prevent unbonding, wrinkling, or shifting that could occur until the bonding agent is completely cool.
3. Add embroidery stitches by hand or machine to further enhance the appliqué. However, fusibles tend to stiffen fabric making hand embroidery more difficult.

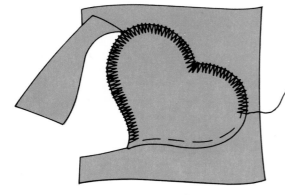

Method One

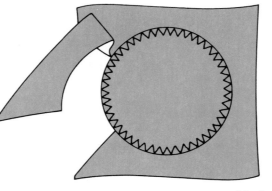

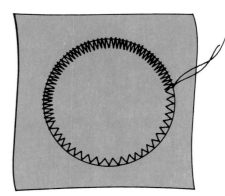

Method Two

Patchwork

Patchwork refers to making a large piece of fabric from small ones. The larger fabric can be made by seaming pieces together (piecework) or by sewing one piece on top of another (appliqué). Today, the terms patchwork and piecework are used interchangably to refer to the seaming together of small pieces. Appliqué and piecework (patchwork) are often used together. An example of the two crafts together is the pillow shown on page 67.

Materials:
☆ Fabrics
   Occasionally silk and woolen fabrics were used, but the traditional patchwork fabric is cotton. Use either cotton or cotton blends in dress or shirt weight fabric. Other possible fabrics are lightweight corduroy and velveteen.

☆ Thread
   For both machine and hand piecing, use cotton-covered polyester thread.

☆ Needles
   Use size 8 to 10 sharps for hand piecing (see page 76).
   Use size 14 machine needle for machine piecing.

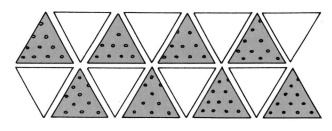

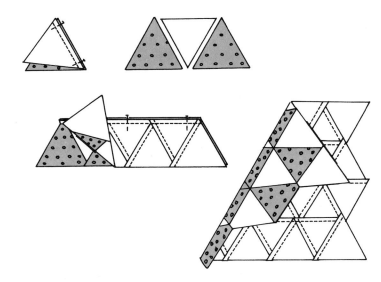

Joining Patchwork Units

Technique:
1. Preshrink and press all fabrics whether newly purchased or scraps.
2. Carefully mark design parts on fabric with either pencil, tailor's chalk, or felt tip marker on the wrong side of the fabric. Lines should be light and thin so use only well-sharpened marking tools. Refer to page 76 for information on making templates for marking and cutting.
3. Cut pieces accurately. Patchwork requires precise measuring and cutting of design elements.
4. Begin by joining one small unit to another. Then, join that unit to another unit and continue until large sections of completed patchwork can be joined.

Piecing by hand:
Use a small running stitch (10 stitches per inch) to piece by hand. Begin with a knot or small backstitch and continue taking three or four running stitches at a time. Backstitch every three or four stitches and end with a backstitch.

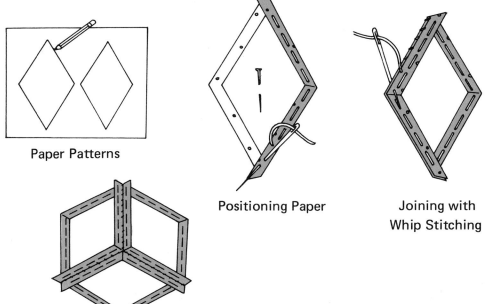

Paper Patterns

Positioning Paper

Joining with Whip Stitching

Joining Completed

For hexagons, parallelograms, and other pieces that have bias edges, paper patterns are helpful in piecing and maintaining the shape. Cut a number of paper patterns exactly the size and shape of the finished patchwork piece. Use construction paper or paper of a similar weight. Center paper pattern on cut fabric and fold seam allowances over paper. Baste through seam allowances, paper, and fabric. Join by holding two pieces with right sides together. Whip stitch along the edge to be joined. Take special care matching and stitching corners. To remove paper patterns, clip basting. The paper patterns can be reused several times.

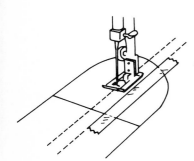

**Masking Tape
Stitching Guide**

Piecing by machine:

Any neutral color thread can be used for the patchwork. Match units, rights sides together, and stitch by machine (10 stitches per inch). Guide pieces carefully with the cut edge against the appropriate seam allowance on the throat plate. Masking tape can be applied to throat plate for stitching guide as shown. Seam allowances of 1/4″ or 3/8″ are most often used for patchwork. There is no need for a backstitch or knot since each seam will be crossed by another seam.

Quilting

Wadded Quilting (English Quilting)

Wadded quilting refers to securing together three layers (top, filling, and backing) with multiple lines of stitches. Quilting may follow the outlines of patchwork or appliqué designs or it may be an independent pattern of its own that covers the entire surface of the piece.

Materials:

☆ Fabric

For the top and backing choose any smooth, closely woven fabric. Cotton is a traditional choice. (Quilt tops are often patchwork or appliqué.) Filling can be polyester or cotton batting (a fluffy non-woven about 1/4″ to 1/2″ thick), several layers of flannel, or polyester fleece. Cotton batting tends to bunch unless it is very closely quilted (a line of quilting every one to two inches). Polyester batting does not bunch and can be quilted with lines farther apart.

☆ Thread

Use quilting thread, #50 cotton thread, buttonhole twist, or cotton-covered polyester. Traditionally, white thread is used for quilting but contemporary quilters use colored threads, too.

☆ Needles

Use any size 8 to 10 sharps. (See page 76.) Some quilters use a curved needle. Try both and choose the one that is the most comfortable and easiest to use.

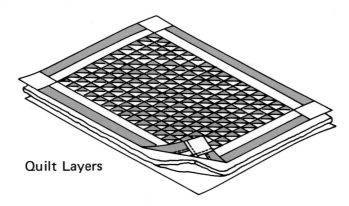

Quilt Layers

Technique:

1. If you are using an allover quilting pattern, mark the fabric by drawing the quilting pattern directly on the quilt top with pencil or chalk.
2. Assemble the quilt. First lay out the backing on a smooth surface with right side down. Smooth batting over the backing. Next, spread the top (right side up) over the batting. Be sure there are no wrinkles in any layer.
3. Pin baste the three layers together using lots of pins. Pin basting is adequate if the quilt will be hand quilted. But, if machine quilting is planned, thread baste layers together. Baste from the center out or in a grid as illustrated.

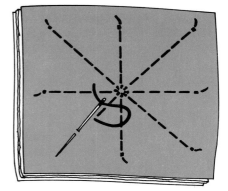

Radial Basting

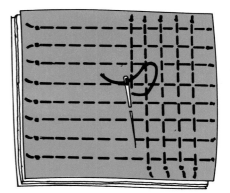

Grid Basting

4. Quilting by hand:

For hand quilting, use a quilting frame or quilting hoop to hold work taut. Traditionally, a quilting frame is used. The quilt is laced to the frame and then is rolled between two beams to progressively expose the unquilted portion until the quilt is finished. Since a quilting frame is almost room size, it is ideal for several people working together but it is not always practical for contemporary quilters as it is not portable. The quilting hoop is similar to an embroidery hoop except that it is larger and sturdier. The quilting hoop is moved from section to section until the quilt is finished. It is lighter and less cumbersome than the quilting frame and is portable. For small quilting projects such as the evening bag with the quilted monogram on page 6, an ordinary embroidery hoop may be used. If your pin basting or thread basting is well done, it is possible to quilt without a frame.

Begin quilting by tying a small knot in the end of the thread and passing the needle through all three layers from backing to top. Tug gently so that the knot passes through the backing into the batting. Take small even running stitches along the marked quilting lines. Stitch with one hand above and one hand below the quilt to be sure the needle goes through all layers. To end stitching tie a knot in the thread close to the fabric surface. Take one more stitch and pull knot into batting. Pass thread off into batting. Bring the needle out and clip thread.

5. Quilting by machine:

After quilt parts are carefully basted together, machine stitch along quilting pattern lines. Use straight stitch, satin stitch, zig-zag, or other decorative stitch. A quilting foot can be very helpful as it rides easily over three layers of fabric and has an adjustable guide for stitching parallel lines without marking.

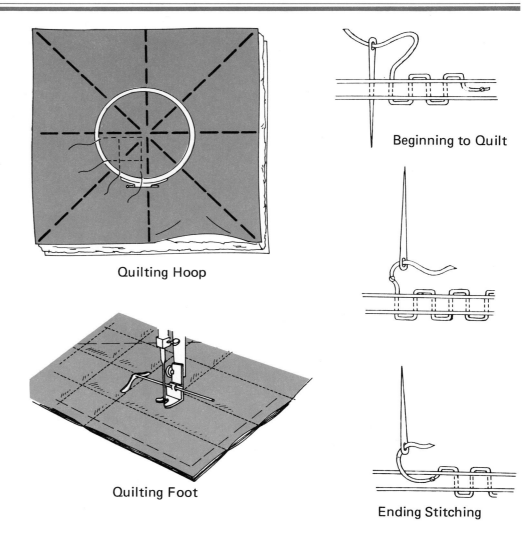

Quilting Hoop

Quilting Foot

Beginning to Quilt

Ending Stitching

Tied Quilting

An alternative to overall quilting is tying. Tying secures the quilt layers with decorative knots, tufts, bows, or buttons. Tying is meant to show and should follow some pattern. See the quilt pictured on page 23 for an example of effective tying.

For tying, thread needle with acrylic or wool yarn, buttonhole twist, crochet thread, or other decorative thread. Pass needle from top to bottom through the layers leaving a tail of thread on top and then up again close to the point of entry. Take another stitch in the same way ending on top. Tie the two ends tightly in a bow, square knot, or other decorative way. Tufting is the same as tying except that an embroidery needle is used with three or four strands of yarn. Yarn ends are clipped evenly to produce the tuft.

Buttons may also be sewn on and finished with tying.

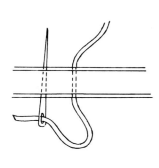

First Stitch

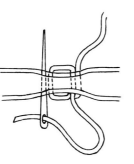

Second Stitch

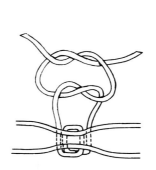

Tying

Adding a Button

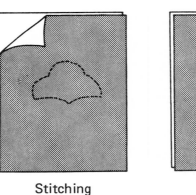

Stitching

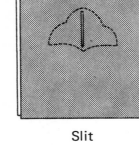

Slit

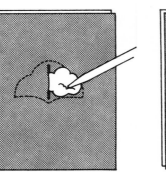

Stuffing

Catch Stitching

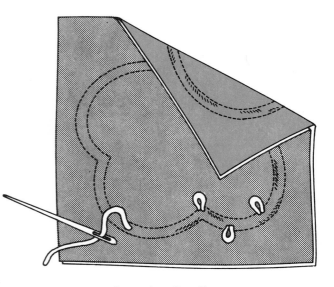

Inserting Cording

Corded and Stuffed Quilting
(Italian Quilting or Trapunto)

Corded and stuffed quilting consists of a design quilted through two layers of fabric and then padded with cording and/or fiberfill to add dimension to the finished product. Stuffing is accomplished by making small slits in the backing fabric. This type of quilting is called shadow quilting when the top layer is a sheer fabric which allows a colorful second layer (backing) to show through in areas that are not corded or stuffed.

Materials:

☆ Fabric
The top layer can be any smooth, closely woven fabric. For shadow quilting use a sheer fabric such as organza, voile, or dotted Swiss. The backing layer can be a smooth, closely woven fabric or cheesecloth. (Do not use cheesecloth for shadow quilting.) For cording, use cotton or polyester, rug wool, or knitting wool. Stuff with polyester fiberfill or batting.

☆ Thread
Use cotton-covered polyester thread.

☆ Needles
For hand sewing, choose size 8 to 10 sharps. (See page 76.) For corded quilting, use a tapestry or rug needle for inserting cording. For machine stitching, use a size 14 needle.

Technique:
1. Press fabrics.
2. Transfer design to wrong side of backing fabric.
3. Layer fabric together so that the marking on the backing fabric is visible. Baste fabrics together.
4. Stitch along design lines by hand (use running stitch, back stitch, or decorative stitch) or straight stitch by machine. Cording requires two parallel rows of straight stitching.
5. Remove basting.
6. Stuff or cord the design areas.
   For stuffing when cheesecloth is the backing fabric, pull a few threads aside; for closely woven fabrics, slit the backing. Push stuffing material into corners and points with a knitting needle.

   Close backing by pushing threads of cheesecloth back together or close the slit with catch stitching. To prevent raveling, a small piece of fusible (iron-on) interfacing may be placed over the slit and fused in place.

For cording select a cord or yarn that will comfortably fill the space between parallel stitching lines. Thread into a tapestry or rug needle. Insert needle into the backing between the rows of stitching. Be sure not to pierce top fabric. To go around a curve, angle, or point, bring needle out and reinsert it at the same place leaving a little cording outside. This prevents puckering or buckling of the work. When completed, trim off all cord ends to about 1/8".

4
The Final Details

Pillow Potpourri

Pillows created from your needlework have personality and warmth far beyond any mass-produced item. There is always room for more pillows because they can be made in many sizes, shapes, and styles and they enhance any setting adding warmth, color and comfort.

Included here are instructions for making two types of pillows, the knife-edge pillow and the box pillow. A knife-edge pillow consists of two sections (top and bottom) sewn together. "Knife-edge" refers to the seam. Variety in this pillow can be achieved by adding cording, ruffles or other trim at this seamline. The common shapes for knife-edge pillows are round, oval, square, and rectangular but the following instructions could be adapted to other shapes, even irregular ones.

To make a knife-edge pillow:
1. Make a pattern for your pillow by drawing two identical shapes the size of the finished pillow. Cut one of these shapes in half for the pillow back. Add 1/2″ seam allowances to the edges of all pattern pieces. Cut pieces from fabric.
2. Stitch the two pillow backs together inserting

zipper following package instructions. Invisible zippers are especially suited to pillows because they are completely hidden in the seam.
3. Unzip zipper. Pin and stitch top and bottom sections of the pillow together. Trim, grade, and clip the seams as necessary.
4. Turn pillow through the zipper opening and press.
5. Stuff pillow to desired fullness. For stuffing alternatives, see page 92.

For a tailored look in pillows, make a box pillow. These are sophisticated, contemporary pillows which can be enhanced with cording, braid, or other trims. The box pillow has a top, bottom, and sides like a box which gives it its name. Box pillows may be made in many shapes, but the easiest to construct are round, oval, square, and rectangular. It is best to purchase a premade foam form for box pillows.

To make a box pillow:
1. Make a pattern by drawing two identical shapes for the top and bottom of the pillow. For the sides of the pillow measure the distance around the outside of the pillow form and draw a straight pattern piece this length and the width of the side of the pillow form. Divide this long piece into

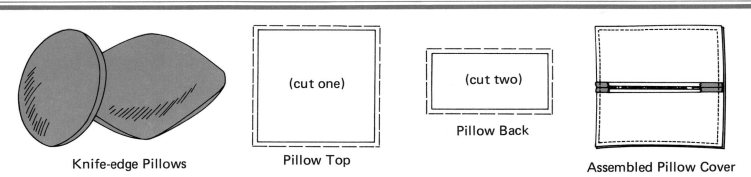

Knife-edge Pillows

Pillow Top
(cut one)

Pillow Back
(cut two)

Assembled Pillow Cover

equal shorter pieces. To use one of these two pieces for a zipper opening, divide it in half lengthwise. Add 1/2″ seam allowances to the edges of all pattern pieces and cut the pieces from fabric.

2. Insert zipper between the two narrow pieces following package instructions. Invisible zippers are an especially good choice for pillow cover closures.

3. Open zipper. Stitch remaining side piece to zipper section and press seams open.

4. With right sides together, pin top and bottom sections to the side section and stitch. Trim and clip seams where necessary and press.

5. Turn pillow cover through zipper opening and insert box pillow form.

Pillow Stuffing Alternatives

Today, thanks to technology and inventiveness, there are several ways to stuff a pillow. Choose the method that is right for your purposes and makes the best-looking pillow.

After the pillow is made it can be stuffed with loose foam or polyester fiberfill. This direct method is quick and easy but the pillow cover is not easily removed for cleaning. If you choose this method, it is not neccessary to insert a zipper in the pillow. Instead, leave a 6″ opening in one of the seams, stuff the pillow, and slipstitch the opening closed by hand.

Another answer is the pillow liner. Liners are simple inner pillows made of muslin or other inexpensive but hard-wearing materials. To make a liner, cut out your pillow pattern in muslin or other inexpensive fabric. Stitch the pillow together leaving a 6″ opening. Turn the pillow and stuff to the desired fullness. Slipstitch the opening. Insert the liner into your pillow cover.

Pillow forms are available today in a range of standard sizes and shapes. Some are polyester and others are molded foam. They combine the ease of direct stuffing with the versatility of the liner. They can be removed easily and are reuseable, but require no construction. When planning to use a pillow form, be sure to work in a standard available size. Odd size pillows require custom-made liners.

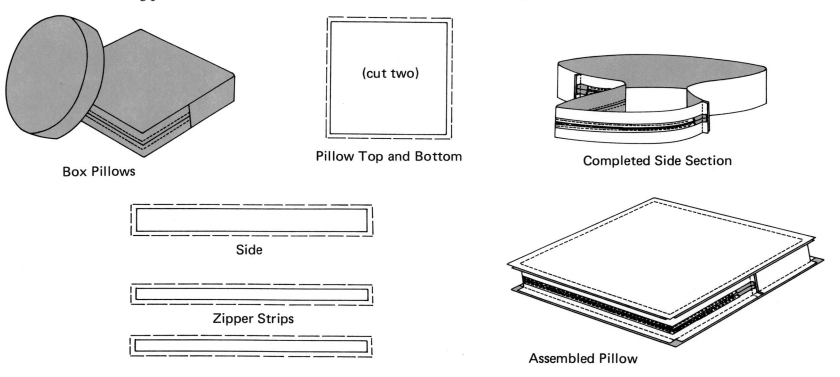

Box Pillows

Pillow Top and Bottom
(cut two)

Completed Side Section

Side

Zipper Strips

Assembled Pillow

Framed Needlework

Wall hangings are used like paintings as provocative, stimulating visual experiences. They may be so important to the mood and scheme of a room that they serve as its focus or may simply add a colorful accent.

Some wall hangings begin in a frame. Working with fabric stretched tautly on a frame is beneficial to certain embroidery, needlepoint, appliqué, and patchwork designs. Other projects that are intended for framing can be stretched after their completion. In either case, stretch fabrics by following these steps. First, assemble artist stretchers available from most art supply stores. Place fabric so that it extends on all sides. Tack or staple each side beginning at the center and working to each corner. Do one side at a time. Fabric should be smooth and taut and the design should be centered and straight. A stretched project can be further finished by framing with a purchased or custom frame or by tacking wood strips or molding to the sides and ends.

The decorative possibilities of enhancing your finished needlework with a frame with or without a mat are astounding because there is such a variety of materials and techniques. Mats are usually made of heavyweight cardboard called mat board which is available in an amazing range of colors and in some textural variations that imitate fabric. Single mats are traditional but in recent years double mats have become the vogue. In a double mat, the top mat is cut slightly narrower than the bottom mat allowing the bottom mat to show as a narrow band of color around the design. An interesting variation is achieved by wrapping pre-cut mats with printed or plain fabric. To accomplish this, cut a piece of fabric the size of the outer dimensions of the finished mat plus at least one inch extra all around. To cover the mat, place fabric face down and center mat on top. Wrap the outer edges of the fabric over the mat and glue in place.

Remove the fabric in the center of the mat leaving an inch on each side. To wrap the fabric around the inner edges of the mat, carefully slash the fabric into but not past the corners of the mat. For an example of fabric-covered mats, see the needlepoint ducks on page 36.

Select mats and frames to reinforce the color, shape, or some other important aspect of the needlework design. The overriding criterion is that mats and/or frames should add to the total effect and never detract attention from the design itself. Making your own frames and cutting your own mats require certain tools, an understanding of precise measurement, and a mastery of certain techniques. The availability of commercially cut mats and custom-made frames is a boon to many crafts people. You might also consider reconditioning an old frame. Auctions, flea markets, garage sales, and antique stores abound with frames that you can refinish to enhance your needlework.

Shops that specialize in matting and framing can be found in almost any city. From their large stock, it is possible to create many framing effects. Such work is costly because of the materials, time, and skill involved, but will assure you of a quality finish for the needlework you spent hours completing. Most shops carry a line of pre-cut, ready-to-assemble frames that are less expensive than custom-made frames, but your needlework must be sized in full inches to take advantage of these frames. Check the yellow pages of your phone directory under "Artist Supplies" to locate one of these shops.

Wall Hangings

The mood and style of some needlework is more suited to a softer "fabric" approach for hanging. For these more casual effects, the fabric is not tautly stretched but is merely finished for convenient hanging. Linings and underlinings provide body so that needlework hangs smoothly. Cording, fringe, and ruffles may be added to finish, decorate, and enhance wall hangings.

One method employs the casing and dowel. Underline the needlework with muslin. Fold fabric edges over the underlining and stitch by machine or hand. Form casing on the top (or top and bottom) by folding a

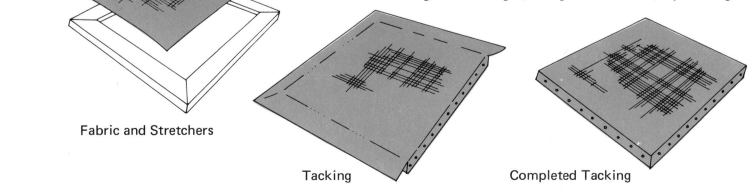

Fabric and Stretchers

Tacking

Completed Tacking

section of fabric to the back and stitching in place. The size of the casing depends on the size rod you intend to use. Line the hanging for a fine finished appearance. Hand stitch the lining over the side and casing edges. Insert a dowel or a decorative rod for hanging.

To hang a needlework project with loops, begin by placing a piece of fabric the same size as the project on wrong side as a lining. Make fabric tubes for the loops or cut strips of felt. Position loops at the top of the project. Finish the edges by stitching fabric strips to the right side of the needlework. Turn strips to the back and secure with hand stitches. Slip a dowel or decorative rod through the loops for hanging.

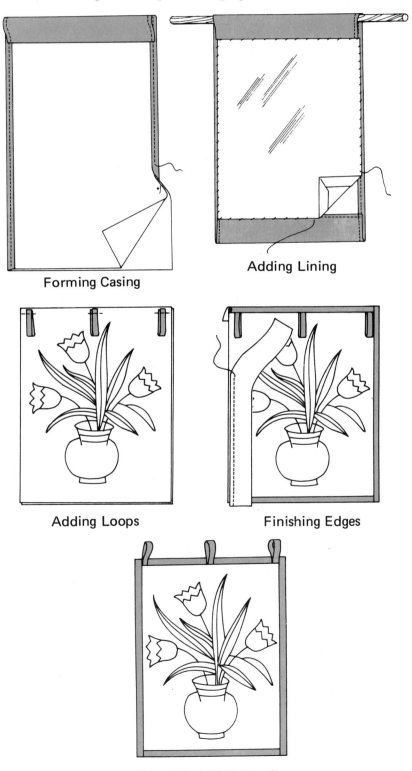

Forming Casing

Adding Lining

Adding Loops

Finishing Edges

Completed Wall Hanging

Backed Needlepoint

Many of the designs included in this book are suitable for interpretation in needlepoint for such things as belts, watchbands, napkin rings, pockets, and coasters. These all have one thing in common—they require backing for a smooth, flat finish. Felt or grosgrain ribbon can be used for this purpose.

To back needlepoint with grosgrain ribbon:
1. Block completed needlepoint (see page 83).
2. Trim excess margin to 1/2″ and turn to back of work. Catch in place with hand stitches that will not show on the right side of the work.
3. Hand stitch grosgrain ribbon over back of work turning under the edges at each end.

To back needlepoint with felt:
1. Complete steps one and two, above.
2. Pin needlepoint to felt right side up and trace around work onto felt.
3. Remove needlepoint and cut out shape just inside traced line so edges of felt will not show on right side of work.
4. Spray surface of felt with a spray adhesive, then position sprayed surface against back of work and let dry. An alternate method is to whipstitch felt to needlepoint.

Professional Mounting

The popularity of needlework has created a need for small businesses which cater to this interest. Many provide finishing and mounting services for completed needlework. These professionals finish pillows, slippers, bookcovers, and many other specialty items. They may also mount and frame needlework pictures and wall hangings.

Shop carefully for such a service since you will be entrusting your time and effort to another person. Ask to see things that have been mounted or finished in the shop. Satisfy yourself that your needlework will be treated carefully. To find persons who do this work, ask in needlework shops, needlework and craft shops in department stores, and check the yellow pages under "Art Needlework."

The Finishing Touch

Time, effort, and planning have been invested in your needlework, and it is worth spending a little extra time to add the perfect finishing touch. It may be a ready-made trim, a piece of antique lace from your grandmother's attic, or a trim of your own creation. Most trims are easy to make and easy to apply. Finishing touches should never compete with the finished needlework but instead they should accent various colors or the mood of the piece. Why not add cording or a feminine ruffle to a pillow or use lace, fringe, or tassels to enhance pillows or wall hangings?

Cording

Cording is a fabric stretched over a cord to create a round trim. It is sometimes also referred to as welting. Cording is often used in the seamline of pillows as an accent and to add strength to the seams. It may contrast, blend, or match the pillow fabric or design.

To make cording, begin by cutting bias strips from fabric. These strips should be wide enough to go around the cord plus an extra 1″ to 1-1/2″ for seam allowances. If you cut the bias strips from a small piece of fabric, it may be necessary to sew several strips of fabric together for a piece of cording long enough to go around the entire pillow. To cut bias strips, start with a rectangular piece of fabric cut on the straight grain. Fold it diagonally, as shown, to find the true bias. Using the bias fold as a guide, mark the fabric with parallel lines the desired width of the bias strips. Mark as many strips as needed, allowing for 1/4″ seams. Mark 1/4″ seamlines on two opposite sides, as shown. Cut strips on marked lines.

To piece strips together, join the short ends of the strips matching the seamlines (not the cut edges), as shown. Pin, stitch, and press seams open. HINT: Cording is available by the yard in a wide array of colors and sizes. It can also be made by covering white cord with fold-over braid, both of which are available by the yard in most notions departments of fabric and department stores.

To complete cording, wrap bias strip or fold-over braid around filler yarn or cord with right sides of the fabric showing. Match raw edges. With zipper foot attachment, machine baste close to, but not on, the filler.

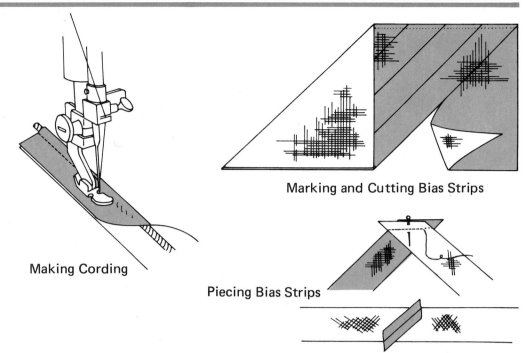

Making Cording

Marking and Cutting Bias Strips

Piecing Bias Strips

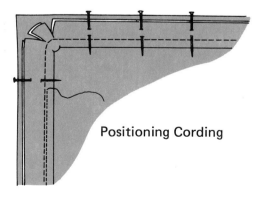

Positioning Cording

To insert cording, position it at the seamline on the right side of the fabric. Machine baste in place with seam allowances of cording matching seam allowances of pillow. Use the zipper foot to stitch close to the cording. To finish cording neatly, overlap and ease the ends of the bias slightly toward the seam edge. Bulk can be eliminated in this area by removing a few stitches at the ends of the cording and then cutting the filler off where the ends cross.

Complete pillow following the directions for assembling pillows. See page 92. Use the zipper foot attachment to stitch the pillow sections together in order to stitch close to the cording.

Ruffles

Ruffles are feminine accents for pillows. They can be wide and soft, or narrow and crisp. They can be used alone or in layers in matching or contrasting colors. Ruffles can be cut on the straight grain or the bias of the fabric. Wide ruffles and ruffles made from sheer fabrics must be quite full to keep them from looking skimpy. You can make your own ruffles following the directions below or you can use any one of the lovely ruffles, flounces, or ruffled laces available by the yard in many fabric and department stores.

To make your own ruffles:
1. Determine the distance around the edges of the pillow cover. Decide how wide the ruffle should be and then cut a strip of fabric the desired width plus 1″ for seam allowance and hem and two to three times as long as the distance around the pillow. It may be necessary to cut several short strips and piece them together into one long strip. If a bias ruffle is desired, see directions for cutting bias strips under "cording" above.

2. Join the two short ends of the ruffle strip and stitch together in a 3/8" seam. Press seam open.

3. Hem one long edge of the ruffle. Turn under 1/4" and stitch close to fold. Turn up 1/4" again and stitch in place by hand or machine.

4. To gather ruffle, machine baste at 1/2" and again 1/4" from the raw edge.

Attaching Ruffle

5. Pin ruffle to the edge of the pillow top at even intervals with right sides together. Draw up the gathering thread to distribute the fullness evenly around the pillow. Machine baste the ruffle to the pillow top on 1/2" seamline.

6. Complete the pillow following the instructions for assembling pillows which begin on page 91.

Fringe and Tassels

Fringe or tassels may be the perfect finishing detail for a pillow or wall hanging made from your needlework. They can be made with any yarn in any weight or texture. To make fringe, cut yarn twice the desired finished length. Fold in half and use a crochet hook to draw loops through fabric. Pull ends through loops and pull tight.

For knotted fringe, cut yarn four times the desired finished length. Insert fringe in fabric as described for fringe, above. For the first row of knots, knot adjacent yarns together across the row. For the second row, pick yarn from each of two adjacent knots and tie together. Continue across the row. After knotting, trim ends evenly.

To make a tassel, cut a strip of cardboard the desired length of the tassel. Wind yarn around the cardboard until the proper fullness of the tassel has been achieved. Thread a needle with a double strand of yarn and slip it through one end of the tassel, as shown. Tie securely, cut the lower loops, and wind the threaded strand around the upper end of the tassel several times about 1/2" from the top. Then slip the needle underneath the wound portion and bring it out at the top of the tassel. Attach tassel to pillow or wall hanging as desired.

For a felt tassel, cut a rectangle of felt and clip it at 1/4" intervals to within 1/4" of one edge, as shown. Roll and secure with stitches.

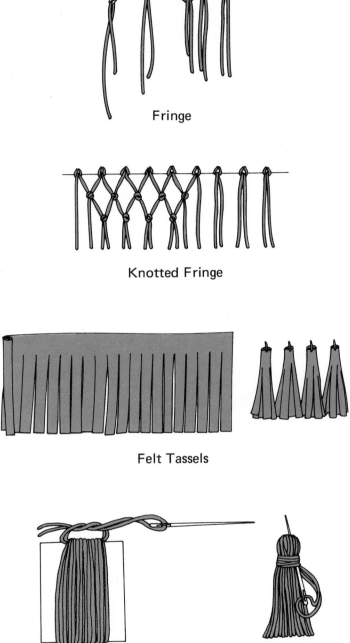

Fringe

Knotted Fringe

Felt Tassels

Yarn Tassel